CONTINUITY
A HISTORY OF THE CATHOLIC CHURCH IN BIRCHINGTON

Author:
CANON WILLIAM CLEMENTS KHS

Published by:
CANON WILLIAM CLEMENTS KHS
Coloma Court, Layhams Road, West Wickham BR4 9QJ

Printed by:
THE CAPITAL PRESS
Lakesview Business Park, Canterbury, Kent CT3 4NH

First Edition Printed July 2010

No part of this publication can be reproduced in any form without the written permission of the Author/Publisher

Copyright © 2010 and all rights reserved

PREFACE

As I put pen to paper, my first intention was simply to begin, as Mr Kevin Docherty did, with the first Mass in Birchington, celebrated by Abbot Erkonwald Egan in 1908.

But when I read Mr Alfred Walker's book, *"The Ville of Birchington"* and saw "The Roman Catholic Church of Our Lady & St Benedict" listed among the various churches and chapels of Birchington as if it were a late arrival on the scene, I decided to go back to the beginning and show the continuity between the faith brought to England by St Augustine, and that shared by Catholics worldwide today.

In so doing, to my surprise, I found that the continuity was more obvious and tangible than I had expected, and was evident from historical records.

I hope you find the whole book interesting, and will feel grateful to all those people, down the ages, who have worked so hard, and, in some cases, suffered so much, to hand on the Good News of the Christian faith to us today.

Canon William Clements

Contents

Part one	Planting the Faith	
	Topography and Early History	10
	The Ville of Birchington	10
	The Roman Invasion	11
	The Coming of Christianity to Britain	11
	The Anglo-Saxon Invasion	12
	The Coming of Christianity to Thanet	12
	Minster Abbey	14
	Monkton	16
	An old Map of Thanet	16
	The Manor of Quex	18
	The Coming of Christianity to Birchington	18
	The Reformation	20
	The Crispes of Quex	21
Part two	A Second Spring	
	A Second Spring in England	26
	A Second Spring in Thanet	26
	The Monks Return	27
	A 13th Centenary Remembered (1897)	28
	Other Christian Churches in Birchington	29
Part three	Our Lady & St Benedict	
	The Birchington Mission	34
	Father Augustine Golding Bird	35
	Father Henry Aldersey, OSB	35
	Father Anselm Spencer, OSB	36
	Father Joseph Power, OSB	36
	Father Alphonse Urban Rouviere, OSB	37
	Father Augustine Keniry, OSB	37
	A Princess at Mass	38
	Father Anscar Charles van Cauwenberghe, OSB	39
	Father Wilfrid Emery, OSB	40
	Father Cyril Williams	48
	Father Kevin St. Aubyn	52
	Father Denis Finbarr Barry	54
	Canon William Clements	57
	A 14th Centenary Remembered (1997)	85
	Our Lady and Saint Benedict Centenary	87
	Our Local Catholic Schools	92
Part four	What of the Future?	
	The Same Church	104
	Christian Unity	107

Part One
PLANTING THE FAITH

1. Topography and Early History

Birchington is a seaside village on the north-east coast of Kent, overlooking the Thames Estuary. It stands on the Isle of Thanet, which in ancient times was separated from the mainland of Kent by a navigable channel composed of the Rivers Wantsum and Stour.

The Wantsum was navigable as late as 1470 AD. A ferry at Sarre is shown on Thomas of Elmham's map of Thanet (1414 AD) and the first bridge there was built in 1485.

Pytheus of Massilina, an early explorer and navigator, visited Thanet in 352 BC and described it as "heavily wooded." Yet archaeologists tell us that from Neolithic times it was a "managed" landscape of field systems, woodland, trackways and settlement sites.

But by the sixth century AD the climate seems to have changed, and battering by wind and sea made life difficult for peasants, as well as causing the gradual silting up of the Wantsum. The huts of mediaeval peasants were made of frail materials- unseasoned rough wood and clay daub – which only lasted a couple of generations. Only the churches were built of stone. Village communities were therefore impermanent. The people were harassed by coastal raiders as well as freak storms; by plague, famine and war. Sometimes they moved on to a roadside location with better facilities for trade. These factors explain why some of the churches of Thanet were abandoned. By 1800 AD nearly all of Thanet was woodland.

2. The Ville of Birchington

Ancient documents refer to the "Ville of Birchington." The word 'ville' is an old Anglo-Saxon/Norman French word for a group of houses with their adjacent land. The name "Birchington" (variously spelt) means a group of houses around a farm on rising ground among birch trees.

Birchington grew up at the crossing-point of two roads – one from Gore End to Minster, the other from Margate to Canterbury. It is recorded that in Birchington there were forty households in 1563. The road to London via Herne Bay and Whitstable came only in modern times. The railway came to Birchington in 1863.

3. The Roman Invasion

Julius Caesar landed at Deal in August 55 BC with a small fleet of galleys. A freak storm forced his withdrawal, but he returned a year later with five legions of soldiers and a large fleet of galleys. His legions crossed the Medway and the Thames, but Gaul, only recently conquered, rebelled, and forced his return there.

It was not until 43 AD, that Aulus Plautius sailed up the Wantsum Channel, and built a fort at Richborough, just beyond Thanet, and seven miles from Birchington, where its remains can still be seen today. Thence began the Roman Conquest, which meant that, for the next 400 years, Britain was part of the Roman Empire.

4. The Coming of Christianity to Britain

The first Christians to come to Britain were probably among the Roman legionaries, and the tradesmen and others who followed them. According to Tertullian and the Venerable Bede, Lucius, King of the Britons, asked Pope Eleutherius in 156 AD to send missionaries to receive him and his people into the Christian church. They and their descendants preserved their faith, even under the persecution of Christians by the Emperor Diocletian in 303 AD. It was during that persecution that St Alban was beheaded in Verulamium. It is recorded that British Bishops of London, York and Lincoln were present at the Council of Arles in 314 AD.

5. The Anglo Saxon Invasion

In 449, AD, as Roman legions withdrew from Britain, Hengist was the first Englishman to land on our shores. He also landed at Richborough. The Anglo Saxon Invasion gradually spread, first in the south, then in the midlands and the north, and the Celtic Christians were pushed to the west.

6. The Coming of Christianity to Thanet

Saint Gregory and Saint Augustine

In 597 Saint Augustine, a Roman monk, landed at Ebbsfleet with forty other monks, sent by Pope St Gregory the Great to convert the English to Christianity. The spot where they landed, about four miles from Birchington, is marked with a Cross erected by Lord Granville in 1884. There they met Saint Ethelred, King of Kent, who though still a pagan, had married a Christian princess named Bertha, daughter of King Charibert of Paris. As Queen Bertha she was given freedom to practice her own faith, and had her own chaplain. With her husband's consent she had built the first Christian church in Canterbury, dedicated to Saint Martin of Tours. Saint Augustine and his monks succeeded in guiding King Ethelbert and his people to faith in Christ.

Augustine erected a monastery to the east of Canterbury on land donated by King Ethelbert. There he died, and was buried, in 604. Gradually the Christian faith spread among East Angles, the West Saxons, the Mid Angles and East Saxons, and on to Northumbria. Under Adrian (669-70) the Abbey became the most important centre of learning in the country.

Saint Augustine's Cross. Erected by Lord Glanville in 1884, on the spot where Saint Augustine and his monks landed in 597

In 669 St Theodore of Tarsus was appointed Archbishop of Canterbury. He was a great organiser, and brought order into the English Church. He centralised the authority of Canterbury, and added ten new dioceses to the seven then existing. He divided the dioceses into parishes, which at first corresponded to the Manors that existed. Local clergy were educated and prepared spiritually in the monastery, and were subject to a long probation, being ordained at about the age of thirty. Some would have been married men.

7. Minster Abbey

Saint Domneva and Saint Mildred

In 670, Princess Ermenburga, great-grand-daughter of King Ethelbert, was given part of the Isle of Thanet by King Egbert, in recompense for his part in the murder of her two brothers. Ermenburga became a nun, and at her profession took the name of 'Eva.' Hence she was known as 'Domna Eva,' or 'Domneva' as we know her today. She built the first monastery at Minster, dedicated to St Mary the Virgin, and was its first Abbess. St Theodore, Archbishop of Canterbury, signed the Foundation Charter.

Domneva was succeeded by her daughter Mildred, who, after her education in France, had joined the community as a nun, made her vow of perpetual chastity before St Theodore, Archbishop of Canterbury, and eventually succeeded her mother as Abbess. By the time she died, some thirty years later, with a great reputation for holiness and kindness to the poor, the community had grown to seventy nuns, and extra accommodation was built for them on the site of the present Minster Abbey.

The Abbey flourished until the Danish invasion, when the buildings were burnt to the ground, and the nuns perished in the flames (about 840 AD).

Mildred was canonised by Pope Urban VI in 1388. She is patron saint of Thanet and her feast day is kept on 13th July.

At the time when Minster Abbey was flourishing, Saint Boniface, a monk from Crediton in Devon, felt a call from God to spread the faith in Germany. He left England in 716 with a band of missionaries, and the nuns of Minster prayed for him and his work and sent gifts of vestments and illuminated manuscripts.

Among the missionaries was St Walburga, a nun from Wimborne, in Dorset, who spent the rest of her life in Germany, and became renowned for her holiness, her kindness and her love for the poor. She became Abbess of the Monastery of Heidenheim, where she died in 779. A hundred years later her remains were transferred to Eichstatt, in Bavaria, where a monastery was built over her tomb – and flourishes today. It was from that monastery that a small band of nuns, threatened with expulsion by the Nazis, came to Minster Abbey in 1937, and are here today, pledged to seek God above all else, and to try to transmit his peace and joy to the people they meet. So, we may say, the circle was completed.

Minster Abbey

As always, the cloistered life of monks and nuns attracts pilgrims, and the nuns of Minster today have a beneficial influence on the parishes of Thanet, including Birchington. Our Candidates for Confirmation regularly visit the nuns for an evening of prayer and discussion. The Junior Parish Council put on a repeat performance at the Abbey of a concert they had organised for the parish. Special Ministers enjoyed supper at the Abbey, with a Talk from Mother Nikola. Each year the nuns invite the whole Deanery to a Mass in honour of St Mildred in St Mary's Anglican Church.

8. Monkton

In 961 Queen Osiva, (Ediva?) widow of King Edward the Elder (son of King Alfred the Great) gave the Manor now known as Monkton to the monks of Christ Church, Canterbury. The parish of Monkton was formed, with responsibility for Birchington and Woodchurch. By 1088 the 'hamlet' of Birchington is mentioned as coming within the parish of Monkton.

Records show that in 1367 Archbishop Stephen Langham instituted Henry de Wootton as Perpetual Vicar in Monkton, with a house and tithes valued at £23 a year. But out of this sum he had to provide for two chaplains or curates for Birchington and Wode. The priest appointed for Birchington was to celebrate Mass "daily if conveniently he could." In the reign of Henry of Henry VIII this curacy was valued at £6 a year.

9. An Old Map of Thanet

About 1414 AD, Thomas of Elmham, a monk of St Augustine's Abbey, Canterbury drew a map of Thanet which showed twelve churches. Those that still exist are All Saints Birchington; St Peter's, St Lawrence (Ramsgate), St John (Margate), St Mary's Minster, Minster Abbey, Monkton and St Nicholas at Wade. Of the other four, only traces remain:-

Woodchurch, Stonar, Sarre (St Giles) and Shuart (All Saints).

Part one | Planting the Faith   *Rev. Canon William Clements* KHS

The map also shows "Parkers," which passed into the hands of the Quex family, and thence to the Crispes (of whom more later). The original map is in the library of Trinity Hall, Cambridge.

10. The Manor of Quex

"Parkers" is shown as a large house on Thomas of Elmham's map. Members of the Parker family, who are the earliest known owners, made bequests to All Saints Church in 1411 and 1418.

The Quex (or Quek) family appear in records as local landowners as far back as 1334. At some point they inherited 'Parker,' probably through marriage, though there is no record of this. But it was John Quek who built the old Manor House of Quex, which survived until 1806. He left a legacy to All Saints Church, and died in 1449.

Three generations later, in the early years of King Henry VIII, Agnes Quex married John Crispe, and the Crispe family owned the estate until 1707, when it was sold. The Crispe family held sway in Thanet from the early 15th century right through until well into the 19th century. They were major landowners, highly respected, and contributed much in the life of Thanet. The Manor of Quex is now owned by the Powell Cotton family whose ancestor, John Powell, purchased it in 1774.

11. The Coming of Christianity to Birchington

There was almost certainly a Saxon chapel on the site of the present All Saints Church, some very early stones of which are visible within the structure of the present building. Between 1150 and 1200, during the reign of King Henry II, the earliest part of All Saints Church, as we know it today, was built. It was recorded as having "three chancels" dedicated to St Nicholas,

St Mary (now the Quex Chapel) and St Margaret (now the vestry) and a tower. During the 14th century, the present nave was rebuilt and the half-aisles were added. People have asked how it was that such a large and splendid church was built in such a small 'hamlet.' The answer seems to be that the Quek family were munificent donors. Memorial brasses can be seen in the church of John Quex, who died in 1449, and Richard, his son, who died in 1459, and of other descendants of the family. There were other benefactors. In 1403, Hamo de Westgate left legacies to the 'lights' of St Mary, St Ann and St Margaret in Birchington Church. Money was also bequeathed at various times for 'watching at the sepulchre, an Easter cloth for the High Altar; repainting of statues, and frankincense.

'Watching at the Sepulchre' refers to what we now call watching at the Altar of Repose – and such watching then continued from after the Good Friday Liturgy until the First Mass of Easter. 'Lights' refers to the illumination of the church, as well as votive candles in honour of Our Lady and the Saints. In the church garden, on the north side, stood a little building called the "Wax House," where they used to make the 'lights' for the church, and for Processions etc. These details are evidence of a thriving love for the Mass, and of devotion to Our Lady and the Saints.

As Mr John Lewis saw it:- "In the time of the Pope's tyrannising here, there were, in the Chapel (Birchington church), besides the High Altar, altars and images and lights maintained for the Blessed Virgin Mary, St Nicholas, the Holy Trinity, St Anne & St Margaret, to which we often find legacies left."

Dr Eamon Duffy, a professor at Cambridge, has argued in his book *"The Stripping of the Altars"* that "late mediaeval

Catholicism was neither decadent nor decayed, but was a strong and vigorous tradition, that the Reformation represented the violent rupture of a popular and theologically respectable system."

Hilaire Belloc called the Reformation "the rising of the rich against the poor". But we cannot deny, and should not deny, that there were abuses within the Catholic Church at that time, and that reform was needed. On the other hand, it cannot be denied that the Reformation in England was politically, rather than religiously, motivated.

12. The Reformation

St John Stone, an Augustinian friar of Canterbury, was hanged there in 1539 for refusing to recognise King Henry VIII as Supreme Head of the Church in England. He was not the first to suffer. Already, three Carthusian monks, and then St John Fisher, Bishop of Rochester, and St Thomas More, Lord Chancellor of England, had accepted death rather than accept the Act of Supremacy, passed by Parliament, which declared the king to be Supreme Head of the Church in England. At the origin of the Church of England lies no theology or Council of the Church, but simply an act of State, an Act of Parliament. Ten years after St John Stone died at Canterbury, the old Catholic ritual was still in use at Birchington. But in 1550, under Edward VI, there was a Visitation by the King's Commissioner, and the High Altar and Lady Altar of All Saints' Church were pulled down, and their cloths sold.

At the succession of Queen Mary in 1553, all the old customs, the Mass, the paschal candle, lamps, statues, candles, incense and the Easter Sepulchre, were restored. Sir Henry Crispe paid for this work, which included the carting of images back from Ashford, where presumably they had been hidden at the time of the King's Visitation.

But this was only for a time. Under Queen Elizabeth I, who was strongly influenced by Lord Cecil, new laws were enacted which made it a treasonable offence for a 'seminary priest' to enter England, and imposed crippling fines for non-attendance at church, where the Book of Common Prayer had been imposed in place of the Mass by the Act of Uniformity in 1559, passed by a majority of only three votes.

13. The Crispes of Quex.

Like many other Catholic families in the land, the Crispes of Birchington had to learn to compromise with this 'Elizabethan Settlement.' Otherwise, not only were they fined, but made ineligible for public office. Some, such as the Crispe family, seem to have chosen occasional appearance at church, whilst retaining the old faith in their hearts, and in their Catholic worship whenever they had the chance. The State called them "Church papists," fellow-Catholics called them "Schismatic" (those cut off). Those who refused to attend church at all were called 'Recusants.'

The Crispe family, as we have noted, were a land–owning, influential and respected family in Thanet, through many generations.

- *Sir Henry Crispe I was Sheriff of Kent. He died in 1575*
- *Sir Henry Crispe II was known as "Regulus Insulae" (Governor of the Island). He died in 1647*
- *Sir William Crispe was Lieutenant of Dover Castle from 1559 to 1572. An historian has written, 'He was a most*

accomplished gentleman and was highly esteemed by the Constable on account of his probity;… kind, liberal and condescending to the poor and indigent, and distributing impartial justice to all." He died in 1576.

Yet, over the next couple of centuries, several members of the Crispe family entered religious orders abroad.

- *Elizabeth, daughter of John Crispe and Kathleen Knatchbull, took the names Sister Mary Stephen as a Poor Clare at Gravelines*
- *Margaret, daughter of John Crispe and Mary Gage, became a Poor Clare at Gravelines.*
- *Mary, daughter of "Henry Crispe of Quex Thanet" and Mary Collins, was professed in 1687 at the convent of the Benedictine nuns in Brussels. She was eventually elected as the 9th Abbess, and died in 1757, aged 87.*
- *Sir William Crispe, Lieutenant of Dover Castle from 1559 to 1572, had eleven children, of whom the youngest, Francesca, married Richard Vincent. Their son William Vincent, was a seminary priest, and died at Ghent in 1660.*

Records show a number of marriages of Crispes into well-known 'recusant' families. From 1574 onwards, priests, ordained abroad, were coming into the country secretly, and moving from place to place, sometimes using an alias, and hiding in the homes of Catholic gentry. It is quite likely that such priests would visit the Crispe family, but there is no evidence of this. By the nature of things, such visits were kept secret from the authorities, though local Catholics would come to Mass and the Sacraments whenever they had a chance. In 1580 a Mr Thomas Deal, of Margate, was reported as keeping in his house a school master who had come from Flanders, had visited Mr Henry Crispe, and did not attend Divine Service at St John's Church. This was probably a seminary priest from Douai, using an alias. All these snippets of information seem to point to an influential Birchington family continuing to hold on to and practise their Catholic faith.

The King's Visitation, as a matter of policy, tried to ensure the rigorous repression of all the externals of Catholicism. Statues and images were to be destroyed, to prevent their being hidden. It was an uphill task for the authorities, with only partial conformity achieved. For a time, there was quiet resistance. In the words of Cardinal Newman, "There was a struggle for a time, then its priests were cast out or martyred. Temples were profaned or destroyed, revenues seized by covetous nobles. The presence of Catholicism was simply removed, its grace disowned, its power despised, its name, except as a matter of history, at length almost unknown. Truth was shovelled away, and there was a calm, a silence, a sort of peace". But through those centuries, from 1570 to 1850, the Church quietly survived. There were no bishops; only, at first, four Vicars Apostolic, one for the London District, doing their best to hold Catholics together and keeping in touch with the Holy See of Rome. The Catholic Relief Act of 1778 allowed Catholics, once again, to inherit or purchase land. Bishops and priests were no longer persecuted, no longer imprisoned for life. The Second Catholic Relief Act 1791, made it lawful to profess and teach the Catholic faith, and to open chapels. The Catholic Emancipation Act 1829 removed most of the remaining restrictions imposed on Catholics. (But still, today, the monarch may not be, nor marry, a Catholic).

Part Two
A SECOND SPRING

14. A Second Spring in England

In 1850, by decree of Pope Pius IX, the hierarchy in England was restored, and Bishop Thomas Grant became the first Bishop of Southwark. On 13th July, 1852 the Bishops were gathered at St Mary's College, Oscott for the first Provincial Synod of Westminster. John Henry (later Cardinal) Newman preached a memorable sermon, the theme of which was "The Second Spring."

In the order of nature, he said, there is perpetual renewal; the sun rising and setting; the seasons of the year; renewal following decay. But in the moral world it is not so; nations, civilisations and empires come and go, never to rise again. Man and all his works are mortal, and have no power of renovation. The majesty of the old Church, which stood in pride of place in England for nearly a thousand years, had been blotted out, never, it seemed, to rise again. The English Church, was, and the English Church was not. But now the English Church "is once again." This was indeed the coming in of a "Second Spring."

It is the theme of this book, as in Newman's sermon, that the Catholic Church in England today, with its hierarchy in union with the Holy See in Rome, is indeed the same Church as that brought to England by St Augustine in 597, and seemingly destroyed for ever by a tyrant state in the centuries following the Reformation.

15. A Second Spring in Thanet

Mass was being celebrated in 1793 in Margate by Father Michael Grundy, chaplain to the Gillow family. In 1801 the few scattered Catholics in Thanet were cared for from Margate by Father Michael Bellesant, succeeded by Father John Jones, Father

Joseph Anson, and in 1822, by Father Thomas Costigan.

Father Thomas Costigan was born in Kilkenny on 24th January, 1788, and educated at St Edmund's College, Ware. Ordained at the age of 29, he was sent to the "Margate Mission" in 1821.

The mission at that time covered the whole of East Kent, as far as Maidstone, Sheerness, Hastings, Ashford, Canterbury, Folkestone and Dover. Father Costigan was a tall powerful man, standing some 6ft 5 inches. He would travel, sometimes on foot, sometimes on horseback, and was known as the "Wandering Apostle." Sometimes, he was pelted with rotten eggs and tomatoes. Father Costigan died on 9th October 1869, and is buried in the monks' cemetery at Ramsgate. His monument there commemorates his 38 years as missionary, friend of his flock and friend of the poor.

16. The Monks Return

When the Catholic Hierarchy was restored in 1850, Bishop Thomas Grant was appointed as the first Bishop of Southwark. His diocese covered South London, Kent, Surrey, Sussex and Hampshire, including the Channel Islands. He wanted Benedictine monks to establish a mission in England, and invited them to Ramsgate. The architect Augustus Welby Pugin had moved to Ramsgate in 1841, and had built a church at his own expense at West Cliff, Ramsgate. It was intended as a model parish church for a small town.

In 1856 Father James Alcock, a member of the Cassinese Congregation of the Benedictine Order, arrived in Ramsgate with a small community, and established a monastery on land purchased from Pugin. They had accepted Bishop Grant's invitation to come to Thanet because of its historic associations. The foundation stone of the Abbey was laid in 1860. In the same year, on the death of Father Thomas Costigan, the monks took over the administration of the Margate mission with pastoral responsibility for the whole of Thanet.

In 1865 they founded St Augustine's College, an independent grammar school for boys. In 1872 Father Wilfred Alcock was elected as the first Abbot of Ramsgate. In 1878 a chapel was established at Broadstairs, and a church was built at Minster in 1901. In 1902 the Church of St Ethelbert and St Gertrude was opened in eastern Ramsgate, and in 1903 a church at Westgate. The first Mass at Birchington was celebrated on 15th August 1908. St Anne's, Cliftonville was opened in 1928, and St Benedict's, Newington, in 1930. There were thus eight Catholic Churches in Thanet, all cared for by the monks of Ramsgate.

Thomas Egan, born in Bedford in 1856, came from Deal as a ten year old boy, and enrolled as a pupil of St Augustine's College. He was a clever scholar, and fond of music and cricket. He became a monk of Ramsgate, taking the name of Erkonwald. He studied in Rome, and was ordained there in 1883. Back in Ramsgate, he was a classmaster, and Head of St Augustine's College for twenty years. In 1906 he was appointed Prior and in 1909 elected as Abbot of Ramsgate. He died in 1939.

Abbot Erkonwald Egan

17. A Thirteenth Centenary Remembered (1897)

To celebrate the 13th centenary of St Augustine's arrival

in Thanet, a Solemn Pontifical Mass was arranged, to take place on the spot at Ebbsfleet where St Augustine landed, commemorated by the stone cross erected a few years earlier by Lord Granville. For the purpose, two special trains were laid on to bring people from London and the suburbs. One train, third class only, left Charing Cross at 7.35 a.m, picked up passengers at St John's, Chislehurst, Orpington, Sevenoaks and Tonbridge, and reached Minster station at 9.50 a.m. A second train, first class only, left Charing Cross at 7.55 a.m, and travelled non-stop to Ebbsfleet, where a special 'viaduct' was constructed to enable passengers to alight close to the site, where a huge marquee had been erected. A 'yellow ticket' costing one guinea, entitled first class passengers also to lunch at the Granville Hotel, Ramsgate and to a return journey at about 6.00 p.m. The date chosen was Tuesday, 14th September 1897. The celebrant of the Mass was Cardinal Herbert Vaughan, Archbishop of Westminster, and the preacher Bishop Hedley of Newport. Also present were Cardinal Perraud, Archbishop of Autun and Canon Bernard, Archpriest of Aix and Arles (all places visited by St Augustine and his monks on their journey to England).

18. Other Christian Churches in Birchington

Baptists | The Baptist Movement goes back to 1609, when a group of 'Separatists', led by Thomas Helwys and John Smyth, (so called for their belief that Church and State should be separate), who had fled to Amsterdam, formed themselves into a congregation, and administered baptism to each other, thus adhering to their belief in believers' baptism. They returned to England in 1612, and founded their first congregation on English soil at Spitalfields in London. The Baptists are first heard of in Birchington in 1740. A corrugated iron chapel was built in c. 1857. The present brick chapel in Crescent Road dates from 1925.

Methodists | The Methodist Church has its origin in the 'Evangelical Revival' of the 18th century in England. John and Charles Wesley were leading figures. They did not aim to create a separate Church, but to revitalise the Church of England. However, the Methodist societies developed a life of their own. Great emphasis was placed on Christian holiness, and Methodists were expected to attend 'classes,' to pray and study together and learn from each other, as well as attending the parish church on Sundays. A formal split from the Church of England took place in 1795. Methodist worship in Birchington dates from 1780, when they hired a Baptist chapel. The present church in Chapel Place dates from 1830.

United Reformed Church | The Bay Free Church was a wooden building dating from 1885. 'Inter-denominational' services were conducted by a Mr Charles Robert Haig. In 1913 this autonomous 'free' congregation joined the Congregational Union. The present brick church dates from 1934. The Congregational Union, dating from 1813, was a union of autonomous congregations which were aiming to follow the Calvinistic reforms of the 16th century, and to live out the Apostolic tradition as recorded in the New Testament. This Union became the Congregational Church of England and Wales, only in 1965. The Presbyterian Church of England grew from groups who had come from Scotland and the Continent, following the same Reforms of the 16th century, but with a stronger centralised administration and control. In 1972 the two Churches combined, and became the United Reformed Church. Later the "Churches of Christ" joined them. An example, perhaps, of a pioneer effort to form one united Church, embracing unity and diversity.

Cornerstone Church | The Cornerstone Church was founded by Pastor David Tidy in 1984 as an Evangelical Free Church, and met in a Youth Club at Cliftonville until they purchased premises in Station Road, Birchington, in 1999. The church closed in 2008.

All Saints Church | It was not until 1871 that All Saints Church, Birchington, was finally granted its independence from its much smaller mother church of Monkton and became an Anglican parish church in its own right. It now has two daughter churches, St Thomas at Minnis Bay (1932) and St Mildred at Acol (1876).

Coptic Orthodox Church | The Coptic Orthodox Church is one of the Ancient Churches of the East which rejected the dogmatic formulation of the Council of Ephesus in 431, and the Council of Chalcedon in 451. Politics, rivalry between the Sees of Antioch, Alexandria and Constantinople, and the interference of the Emperor, together with confusion over language and terminology, all contributed to the misunderstanding, and in 451 the Church of Alexandria followed the excommunicated Patriarch Dioscoros into schism. In 1973 Pope Paul VI, Bishop of Rome, and the Coptic Orthodox Pope, Shenouda III, signed a Joint Statement affirming their common faith in Jesus Christ our Saviour, true God and true Man.

In August, 1992, a Coptic Orthodox priest, Father Axious, celebrated their liturgy for the first time in the Church of Our Lady & St Benedict, and this continued monthly for six years until, in 1999, a redundant Methodist Church in Cliftonville was purchased, and consecrated on 14th August, 1999, by Pope Shenouda III, who came from his home in Cairo for that purpose. Father Angelos Elantony, and some of his scattered flock, live in Birchington, and Father Angelos is a member of the Birchington Clergy Fraternal.

Churches Together in Birchington | There are nowadays good relations between the various Churches of Birchington, though they all maintain their separate identities. Ministers meet every couple of months for prayer, discussion and planning together, followed by luncheon. Inter-denominational Study Groups are organised during Lent each year, there is a Joint Carol Service, during Advent, and a Good Friday procession from all the churches to Dog Acre for a short service. We have all visited one another's churches for an explanation of our beliefs and customs.

Part Three
OUR LADY
and
ST BENEDICT

19. The Birchington Mission

Until 1908, Birchington had been part of the parish of Margate. On 15th August 1908, the Feast of the Assumption of Our Lady, Birchington was formed as a separate Mission, and Prior (later Abbot) Egan celebrated the first public Mass in Birchington in modern times. It was celebrated in the 'Institute,' a building at the rear of the north side of the Square. This building had been acquired by the villagers, with the help of the first Vicar of Birchington, Rev J Alcock, and several like-minded villagers. All kinds of meetings were held there, and it was, in effect, the first Village Centre. A large Public Hall was opened in 1902, and thus the Institute became a second Hall, and was made available to local Catholics for their first Mass. The site was roughly behind where 'Brills Hardware' shop now stands.

The Original (a converted wagon shed)

The monks of Ramsgate, on 8th September 1908, the Feast of the Birthday of Our Lady, purchased a piece of land, next to the Old Malthouse, which included a wagon shed consisting of three low brick walls and a corrugated iron roof, open at the front to allow wagons to be backed in. The front was closed, doors and window were fitted, and this became a temporary church, which Prior Egan solemnly blessed during Mass on

8th December 1908, the Feast of the Immaculate Conception. By the following May a presbytery was completed, and Father Augustine Golding Bird moved in as the first priest-in charge of the Birchington Mission. Two months later, on 9th February 1909, Bishop William Brown, Vicar General of the Southwark Diocese, granted him a faculty to erect Stations of the Cross, with all the indulgences granted by the Holy Father to those who make the Stations.

20. Father Augustus Golding Bird

Father Golding Bird was an Oblate of Saint Benedict. He remained in charge of the Birchington Mission until 5th February 1912. For the rest of the year there was no resident priest, but Father Athanasius Avignon, priest-in-charge at Westgate, looked after the new Birchington Mission until Father Henry Aldersey was appointed to Birchington in 1913.

21. Father Henry Aldersey OSB

Father Aldersey made his profession as a monk in 1904, and was ordained in 1910. He was appointed to Birchington on 1st January 1913 and saw the local community through the difficult days of the First World War. Owing to poor health, he relinquished the task in 1919. He died on 11th November 1924, and is buried in the monks' cemetery at Ramsgate.

Father Henry Aldersey OSB outside the Church Porch

22. Father Anselm Spencer OSB

The next priest-in-charge was Father Anselm Spencer, who took over in December 1919

Born in London in 1859, he was ordained at Oscott College in 1884 as a secular priest. Four years later, he joined the Benedictine community at Fort Augustus as a novice, and was eventually professed. For health reasons, he moved to Ramsgate, and was appointed to Birchington in December 1919. Three months later he moved into the care of the Daughters of the Cross at Hayle, in Cornwall, where he died on 26th March 1924, and is buried.

23. Father Joseph Power OSB

Father Joseph Power was born in Birchington in 1857, and entered the Benedictine Order in Ramsgate in 1879. After studying philosophy and theology in Rome, he was ordained to the priesthood on 22nd August, 1886, and then taught in Saint Augustine's College for eight years.

In 1902 he was placed in charge of the newly established Mission of Sts Ethelbert and Gertrude at Ramsgate. This was followed in 1906 by his appointment as Chaplain to a Convalescent Home for Children in Margate, run by the Daughters of the Cross. During the next twelve years he endeared himself greatly to these sick children, but was forced by ill health to resign the post in 1918, when he became an invalid himself.

In the Spring of 1919 he was sufficiently recovered to take over the Mission of Birchington, where he worked until his death there on 6th February, 1921. His grave is in the monks' cemetery in Ramsgate.

24. Father Alphonse Urban Rouvière OSB

Born in 1859, he entered the Monastery of Pierre-qui-Vire in France in 1879, and took simple vows in Paris in 1881. He then came to England, and was solemnly professed at Buckfast Abbey, and ordained there in 1884. Having joined the Ramsgate community, he served at Birchington from February 1921 to December 1925. He died on 2nd November 1959 at the age of 80, having been a monk for sixty years.

Church interior in the 1920s

25. Father Augustine Keniry

As a monk of Buckfast, Father Augustine Keniry was 'lent' to Ramsgate, and eventually elected into that community. He was priest-in-charge at Birchington from December 1925 to January 1933. He was then moved to the newly established Mission at Cliftonville. He died on 26th September 1961, and is buried in the monks' cemetery.

Church & Presbytery in the 1920s

Very little information exists regarding life in the mission of Birchington in those early years. But from 1931 the Thanet Catholic Review, published by the monks of Ramsgate, contained occasional references to Birchington.

26. A Princess At Mass

You never know who may be kneeling next to you at Mass in church. On 19th October 1931, Princess Orietta Amelia Maria Doria Pamphilj Landi, aged nine, was confirmed in Our Lady & St Benedict Church by Archbishop Peter Amigo. With her parents, Prince Filippo and Princess Gesine Mary Doria Pamphilj Landi, she stayed regularly with her aunt, Miss Dykes, a parishioner, who was princess Gesine's sister. On 12th November 1933, Prince Filippo and Princess Gesine stood as Sponsors for a number of children who were confirmed by Bishop William Brown.

At the end of the Second World War, Princess Orietta, now in her twenties, and working as a volunteer in a Catholic Women's League canteen at the Adriatic port of Ancona, met Sub-Lieutenant Frank Poyson of the Royal Navy, and invited him to her house in Rome during his Christmas leave, giving the address as 304 via del Corso, and describing it simply as a 'big old house.' It turned out to be the Palazzo Doria Pamphilj, a Baroque palace of more than a thousand rooms.

When Prince Filippo died in 1958, Princess Orietta, as his only child, inherited all his vast estates, with their titles and responsibilities. She was the last survivor of one of Europe's greatest families, with Pope Innocent X as one of her ancestors. Frank Pogson and Princess Orietta were married in Brompton Oratory in 1958. Having no children of their own, they adopted two children from a London orphanage, whom they named Jonathan and Gesine.

Following the reforms of the Second Vatican Council, the Princess and her husband, both devout Catholics, worked to promote better relations between Christian denominations. The Anglican Centre in Rome, based in the Palazzo Doria Pamphilj, was visited by our own Queen Elizabeth in 2000. Frank was for many years a Director of the 'Tablet.' He died in 1998, and Princess Orietta in 2000. Under Italian law, orphans, Jonathan and Gesine have inherited equal shares in all the vast family estates, with their titles and responsibilities.

27. FATHER ANSCAR CHARLES VAN CAUWENBERGHE OSB was born at Courtrai in Belgium in 1868. Universally known as "Father Charles," he entered the Benedictine monastery of Steenbrugge as a novice at the age of 16, and was ordained to the priesthood in 1895. In 1921 he was awarded the Medal of King Albert for his charitable work for the suffering people of Belgium during the First World War. He was later invited to Ramsgate for a time as cantor, though his superiors warned him that he "would never get on with those English." Nevertheless he stayed in England for good. Having served for seventeen years as priest-in-charge at St Ethelbert's, Ramsgate, he came to Birchington in 1934.

Father Charles

In 1940 the Ministry of Security issued a blanket order for all 'foreigners' to leave coastal areas of south-east England. When a young constable respectfully served on him the order of expulsion, Father Charles reduced him to blushful incoherence by responding, "Foreigner! Young man, I have been in Thanet longer than you." For the remaining years of the War the mission virtually closed down, and numbers at Mass were very depleted, as many people had left the area because of the threat of air raids. During those years a Mass on Sundays and Holydays was provided from Margate parish. At the end of the war Father Charles returned to Birchington, and carried on, in spite of his age and infirmities. The people had returned, and on 17th May 1953 Bishop Cyril Cowderoy confirmed 38 candidates, of whom eleven were from Birchington. The congregation overflowed into the porch and the Hall. In 1954 Father Abbot surprised Father Charles by informing him that, at the age of 86, the work of serving Birchington was too much for him. He died on 20th February 1960, in Bon Secours Nursing Home, and is buried in the monks' cemetery at Ramsgate.

Father Wilfrid Emery, OSB

28 Father Wilfrid Emery, OSB

Father Wilfrid was born in 1901 at Clifton, in Bedfordshire. He was received into the Catholic Church at Margate in 1922. A year later he entered Ramsgate Abbey as a novice, and was professed in 1927. His studies at Sant' Anselmo in Rome gave him a love for Italy. He was ordained at Montevergine in July 1932. He had an ardent love for the liturgy of the Church, and applied his artistic skills to the furnishing of our church, and to the making of sacred vestments, some of which are still in use in our church today. One of our parishioners, Mrs Elizabeth Taylor, helped him for many years in making vestments.

Father Wilfrid was sent to Birchington on 14th November, 1954. The Abbot had charged him to "go and build a new church in Birchington," and this led Father Wilfrid ruefully to meditate on Chapter 68 of the Rule of Saint Benedict, which is entitled "If a monk is ordered to do the impossible." It was forty-six years since the temporary church of Our Lady & Saint Benedict was established. It was Father Wilfrid's achievement that a new and permanent church replaced it. Things moved quite quickly. A fortnight after his arrival, Father Wilfrid met a number of gentlemen to discuss plans for the development of Catholic life in Birchington. A week later he met the ladies.

At both meetings, his plans were approved, and everyone promised wholehearted support. His plan was to build a new church around, up and over the existing church, and then remove the old building, in such a way that services continued, uninterrupted.

The new sanctuary

Father Wilfrid began by building a new sanctuary, and an enlarged porch. These were completed by 1955. The sanctuary was simple, beautiful and uncluttered; the altar, a simple 'mensa' (table) had a damask silk frontal, and on it, around the tabernacle, were six brass candlesticks and a simple crucifix. Above the altar was a 'tester' (a gilded wooden canopy) to emphasise the Divine Presence. The sanctuary was liturgically correct, and facilitated worship according to the Tridentine Rite. Thus it was that, for the Patronal Feast that year, the

Abbot of Ramsgate was able to celebrate the first Pontifical High Mass ever held in Birchington. He was assisted by Fathers Odilo Frelinx, Dunston Pragnell and Gregory Rees. A large contingent of monks provided the choir, with Father Stephen Holford at the organ. The parish altar servers, guided by Father Bede Winslow, were commended. Major C O'Connor, chaplain to the United States Air Force personnel based at Manston, was especially welcomed, and the contact proved very fruitful as work on the new nave commenced. The USA Strategic Air Command at Manston comprised, until 1950, the 20th Fighter Bomber Wing, then, until November, 1951, the 12th Fighter Escort Wing; then until 1958, the Kentucky Air National Guard, with their families. These were first called the 123rd Fighter Bomber Wing, but, from July 1952, re-designated as the 406th Fighter Interceptor Wing of the Third Air Force.

For three years these American airmen worked alongside Father Wilfrid and two local builders on the building of the new nave 'round and over' the existing walls, which were then demolished. When completed, the new walls were ten feet higher than the old. During the time that the US Air Force were stationed at Manston, Father Wilfrid had assisted the Air Force Chaplains, and they and the personnel had shown practical interest in, as well as financial support for, the development of the Birchington Mission. Their departure in 1958 was a source of mutual regret.

At Easter, 1956, Father Wilfrid thanked, among others, George Downar, the organist, and John Mann, who gave valuable help during the ceremonies of Holy Week and Easter. On 5th July, Bishop Cyril Cowderoy made his Canonical Visitation and administered Confirmation. The building programme was sufficiently advanced to make, not only the Sanctuary, but also the Sacristy, Confessional and adjacent rooms, available for use.

In his address the Bishop passed in review the vicissitudes of the parish and the plans for its development. It was in moving terms that he expressed his delight in the progress both spiritual and material that has been made in the past eighteen months. After recalling the conditions which formerly prevailed, and which could have caused many to despair, he praised both priest and people for their zeal and generosity by which so much had been achieved in so short a time. The sanctuary was beautiful, he said, and foreshadowed the type of the rest of the church when it should be completed. His Lordship thanked all who had in any way contributed to the work: in particular Rev Father (Major) T Higgins USAF., and the American Catholics of Manston under his care, as well as those personal friends of Father Wilfrid from outside Birchington. He also expressed his (and our) grateful appreciation to Mr Longley and Mr Emmerson who had carried out the construction so satisfactorily and at so reasonable a cost. The Bishop promised his utmost support in completing the task.

By 1957, Father Wilfrid was thanking everyone that work costing over £2000 had been carried out without going into debt. He now planned to extend the nave, to build a new porch, and even a 'Jubilee Tower.' At the same time he had to face the need to re-roof the church, at a cost of a further £1000. In 1958, the extension of the nave was begun and completed. That summer, work was commenced in the new porch, which was to form the base of the Tower.

When the extended nave was completed, the walls of the whole nave and the sanctuary were covered, to a height of ten feet, with beautiful Japanese Oak panelling. Whilst all this structural work was in progress, Bazaars and Summer Sales helped to provide funds for the various improvements. There were also some notable gifts.

Messrs Elliot and Son, of Ramsgate, presented the church with a marble font. An anonymous donor gave the Calvary, which

Construction of Church Tower. 9th September, 1960

was placed at the entrance drive, and solemnly blessed on 18th September 1955. A gift of oak pews replaced the existing seating in the nave. Communion Rails in memory of Leonard King (these are now the altar servers' kneelers).

A carpet was donated in memory Rhoda Toogood. A screen and bench at the back of the church were a thanksgiving from Mr J H P Bryant. Other gifts included four oak prie-dieux. Two fine groups of figures of the Holy Family, carved in oak, commissioned by Father Charles, were installed. They are original works, carved by A de Nys of Belgium. One showing Jesus being taught carpentry by St Joseph, is still in our church. The other, showing the finding of the Boy Jesus in the Temple, was later, at the request of Mr Eddie Hughes, the Headmaster, moved to St Gregory's Primary School in Margate.

The bronze doors to the porch, designed by J Francis Coote, and made by Messrs Blunt and May of Clerkenwell, were donated by a generous friend of Father Wilfrid. The mosaic over those doors was designed by Monica Cowell, a gifted local artist. Her full-size water colour was sent to Rome, and Francesco Vignanelli (who had been responsible for the mosaics and sculptures in the rebuilding of Monte Cassino after World War II) turned the design into mosaic in his Rome studio. Thence it was transported to England, and fixed in position by two young Italian workmen, sent over to do the job. The mosaic depicts Our Lady of Montevergine and Saint Benedict, with the words, 'Domus Dei et Porta Coeli.' (House of God and Gate of Heaven). Its gold and rich colours have stood the test of time.

When congratulated on completing the rebuilding of the church, Father Wilfrid said that there was still much more to be done – a stone altar, a clock and a peal of bells in the Tower, and a new entrance road and car park. It is noticeable that, at each step in all the work on the church, Father Wilfrid remarks, "All is paid for." He must have been a good money-raiser!

In 1959 the Bishop made the following comments in his Visitation Report:- "Your extension and beautifying of the church is beyond all praise, and you have carried through this fine work without contracting a debt. You have had generous help from the Catholic Americans at Manston, but a large measure of praise must go to you for your own efforts to raise money, and the unselfish and moderate way in which you live. I am deeply grateful to you. What you have accomplished is a model of what can be done with effort and imagination even in a very small and poor parish. It is a real joy to visit such a parish."

Later that year, in his Rosary Sunday Letter to the Diocese the Bishop wrote:-

"At Birchington the extension and beautifying of the Church of our Lady and St Benedict has been so considerable as to provide what is in fact a new and very charming church: and thanks to the hard work of priests and people this has been accomplished without contracting a debt."

Church exterior in the 1960s

By the time of the Bishop's next Visitation in 1962, a high altar in Portland stone was ready for consecration, and a new electrical installation was in place in Church, Hall and Presbytery.

The Church and its new altar were solemnly consecrated by Bishop Cyril Cowderoy on 14th July 1964. His Lordship expressed his appreciation of such a delightful little church in its attractive setting. The Abbot of Ramsgate and a choir of monks were joined by many neighbouring prelates and clergy. Afterwards, all enjoyed excellent refreshments in a grand marquee erected for the occasion.

Early in 1963 Father Wilfrid and the people were distressed by the theft of the figure of Christ from the Calvary. This was one of five acts of sacrilege in the churches of Thanet at that time. A new figure was made in memory of Mr Denis Kinsella, who had given the original Calvary.

A Miller organ was the first of the improvements made from the legacy of Dolores Chetwynd, who had died in 1965, and who is commemorated by a stone plaque in the church porch.

On 28th May, 1965, the new Province of Southwark was formed, with Arundel and Brighton, Portsmouth and Plymouth as Suffragan Sees. Bishop Cyril Cowderoy, thus became Archbishop and Metropolitan.

At his visitation on 16th May 1967 His Grace the Archbishop praised Messrs R Petts for their fine stone and marble work, and Messrs Butterworth for their elegant metal work. Later that year Mr Ronald Stone embellished the side door of the church with copper cladding, including the Papal arms and a quotation aptly chosen, from the prophet Haggai:-

Magna erit gloria domus istius novissimae plus quam primae. (The new glory of this house is going to surpass the old).

[Historical note:- The first Jews to return from the Babylonian Exile to rebuild the Temple in Jerusalem were quickly discouraged, and the short prophecy of Haggai, dated 520 BC, stirred them to new efforts].

These records speak mostly of material progress, but the Church is people rather than buildings. Such progress was only possible with the enthusiastic support of the people. Mention is made in the records of a Conference of the Society of St Vincent de Paul, covering the two parishes Birchington and Westgate and dating from 1912. This society of Catholic men was founded in Paris by a student, Frederic Ozanam, in 1833, to relieve the spiritual and corporal necessities of the destitute. It is now open to women.

The Union of Catholic Mothers is a National organization of Catholic married women who aim to follow the full Christian ideal of marriage and home life. A local branch of the UCM was set-up in Birchington about 1955, and consisted mainly of young mothers whose children attended St Gregory's School. Presidents over the years have included Joyce Dowling, Beryl Lind, Joan Ryan and Monica Moulsdale. Father Wilfrid recorded their help with bazaars, fêtes and children's parties.

In January, 1969, Father Wilfrid gave-up the charge of Birchington, and became chaplain at Les Oiseaux Convent, where the Canonesses of Saint Augustine were running an independent boarding and day school for girls. A presentation was made by parishioners, in appreciation of his fourteen years of devoted and loyal service to the parish. Later that year, the Archbishop, on his Visitation, paid tribute to the devoted work of Father Wilfrid, and laid special stress on the tremendous debt the people of Thanet owned to Ramsgate Abbey. In 1969 Miss Rhoda Toogood and Mrs Balderston, two devoted parishioners, died and left legacies to the church.

Father Wilfrid died on 16th March, 1989. He is buried in the monks' cemetery in Ramsgate.

29. Father Cyril Williams

Father Cyril Williams was born in Cleethorpes in 1925. He studied for the priesthood at St Joseph's College, Mark Cross, and St John's Seminary, Wonersh, with a break during which he qualified as a Mental Nurse. Cyril Williams was ordained

Father Cyril Williams

by Archbishop Cowderoy on 30th May 1953. The 'Wonersh 1953 Class', of ten, along with Cyril, included Bill Clements and two future bishops, Howard Tripp and Frank Walmsley. After ordination, Father Williams served as curate at Addiscombe and Balham. When Father Wilfrid resigned in 1969, Archbishop Cowderoy looked for a priest with zeal and energy, to replace him as the first secular priest in Birchington, and chose Father Williams. His first year at Birchington was a crowded one. Having taken a census, he visited almost all known Catholic families by the end of the year. He started a 10.00 a.m Mass on Wednesdays, an Evening Mass on First Fridays, an extra Mass at 10.00 a.m on Holy Days of Obligation, and Benediction once a month. All these proved very successful.

The membership of the Union of Catholic Mothers trebled, a Parish Committee was set up, and a number of social occasions arranged – coffee mornings, whist drives, jumble sales, talks on local history, First Communion breakfasts, a very successful garden fête, and an equally successful bazaar. The final social activity of the year was a parish dinner and dance at the Bungalow Hotel in November (now replaced by Bierce Court.). A strong and active Social Committee was formed, and a special Committee for youth was inaugurated.

During 1971 the Sisters of the Holy Family gave up their convent in Ramsgate, and presented their statue of Our Lady of Lourdes to Birchington. It had stood in their garden since 1954, when it was blessed by Bishop Cowderoy. Father Williams himself built a grotto for the statue in the church grounds, where it stands today. The statue was recently (2007) restored and beautifully repainted by Allison Moores.

There is an impressive list of repairs, redecoration, improvements and acquisitions during 1969. The carved wood statues of Our Lady and St Joseph, presented by Patricia Elliott, are still there today. An oak altar, for Mass with the priest facing the people, was made locally at a cost of £84.

But the roof of the church was leaking and threatening to damage the lovely Japanese oak panelling installed by Father Wilfrid. In March 1969, Messrs Palmer and Reading, a Bexley firm of surveyors, submitted a six page report on the state of the church roof, revealing severe faults in its construction, and suggested that, in the long term, the roof should be replaced.

About this time, the Archbishop had appointed Messrs Stanley Hicks & Son as Diocesan Surveyors, and had encouraged parish priests to engage their services for a survey of all parish properties. Father asked them for a Report on the church, presbytery and hall in Birchington. The Report dated December 1969 was devastating. The construction of the church, bit by bit over the years, was, it said, fundamentally defective, and further expenditure on it could not be justified. It would be better, and cheaper, to rebuild the church.

The church roof, of crudely constructed light-weight trusses, forming a simple pitched roof behind the parapets, was covered with corrugated asbestos. The gutters were narrow, shallow, and inadequate, and the roof would have to be replaced, as its structure was wholly bad. The walls were badly constructed without damp courses, uneven and bulging in places, and this raised the question of whether they would be strong enough to bear a new roof. It would be possible to construct a new roof carried on steel or reinforced concrete columns outside the existing main walls. A very approximate estimate of the cost would be between £10,000 and £12,500 at that time. However, the only proper and, in the end, cheaper solution would be to build a simple modern church. The presbytery needed immediate attention to a problem of rising damp and wood rot, but otherwise was in a reasonable state for a building of its age. The Hall was a temporary timber building, lined with hard board, and was at the end of its useful life. The report on the church caused consternation in the parish, and was reported in the East Kent Times, the Isle of Thanet Gazette and the Universe.

One headline read, "Shock Report dooms £30,000 church," and the article emphasised the fact that so much money had been spent on beautifying the church, and that it had been solemnly consecrated only six years earlier. Father Williams and Father Wilfrid were both interviewed by the press. Father Williams told them that it would be premature to make any predictions about the future of the church. The survey would have to be studied by himself and his superiors, and only then would a decision be made. The people also had their say, and the Report was, in effect, set aside, so far as the future of the church was concerned. However, a new Hall was built, and the presbytery eventually replaced. Father Williams had in mind that, if at some future time the church had to be demolished, Mass would be celebrated in the Hall whilst a new church was being built.

The new Hall was completed in 1973. Entrance was from the church porch to a 'narthex' or ante-room, from which there was access to toilets, kitchen and a small bar, as well as to the

Hall itself, with room for 150 people. These facilities led to the enthusiastic formation of St Benet's Social Club, with a licensed bar. A pair of garages was built adjoining the Hall, and the total cost was £19,349.60.

Yet, at the beginning of 1972, Father Williams' laconic comment in the *Thanet Catholic Annual* read:- "Nothing of note happened last year- just the usual steady grind of a very loyal, very active and very hard-working parish." Of 1972, he simply wrote, "an uneventful but very satisfactory year." Of 1973 he noted "the building and opening of a small parish hall," and added "Despite this, parish activities have gone on as smoothly as ever." These are surely masterpieces of understatement!

In the mid 1970's, a group of girls including Bernie Mann and Marisa and Suzanne Yeo, served coffee in the Hall each Sunday after the 10.30 a.m Mass. Towards the end of his time as parish priest of Birchington, Father Williams, with the help of a loan provided by the Diocese, purchased a bungalow at 12 Sussex Gardens, for use as a presbytery, and the old presbytery was demolished. Just before Christmas, 1975, Father Williams announced that the Bishop had asked him to move to Deal as parish priest. He also became Officiating Roman Catholic Chaplain to the Royal Marines based at Deal, and was eventually appointed Dean of the Dover Deanery. He retired in 1992, and now lives in Whitstable.

30. Father Kevin St Aubyn

Father Kevin St Aubyn was born in Walworth, and baptised in the Chapel-of-Ease of St Alban in Herring Street. The family moved to Redditch in Worcestershire, and Kevin became a boarder in the college of the Sacred Heart Fathers (of

Fr Kevin St Aubyn

Betharram) at Droitwich. At 16, Kevin tried his vocation in their novitiate, but left eventually to join the RAF. After National Service, he entered St John's Seminary, Wonersh, and was ordained on the 11th June 1960. He served as Assistant Priest at Hove, Tooting Bec, Worcester Park and Putney. During those years he qualified as a civil airways pilot. He also obtained a Degree in the Social Sciences.

On 11th December, 1975, Father Kevin became Rector of the Birchington Mission, just a few days after Father Williams had purchased a bungalow at 12, Sussex Gardens, for use as a Presbytery. It took nine months to furnish it and install new windows and a heating system, and to repair the electrical installation, and thus to make it a reasonably comfortable and efficient presbytery. Joan Ryan was a great help to him at this time. Meanwhile, Father Kevin lived in the old condemned presbytery, and had to go to the homes of parishioners to have a bath! He moved into Sussex Gardens on 8th September, 1976.

On Easter Sunday, 18th April, 1976, the Mission of Birchington was, by decree of Archbishop Cyril Cowderoy, raised to the status of a parish, and Father Kevin became the first parish priest, being inducted by the Dean, Abbot Gilbert Jones. On coming to Birchington, Father Kevin was pleased to find an Advisory Council, a flourishing UCM chaired by Joan Ryan, and an active Social Club, with a good social life in the parish. All these he encouraged and supported with enthusiasm. There was a good group of young altar servers, able to carry out the Holy

Week ceremonies in a dignified manner. At Saturday Evening Mass, Paul Keenan served regularly, and someone commented that, with his dignified bearing, he looked like the priest, with Father Kevin as the server! Father Kevin himself was insistent that ceremonies should be liturgically correct. It was he who first arranged for adult members of the congregation, and not just the altar servers, to be Readers at Mass.

The Union of Catholic Mothers was responsible for organising the first Women's World Day of Prayer to take place in our church. Sister Immaculata, a Franciscan Missionary Sister who was a 'regular' on Southern Television was the guest speaker.

The building of the new Parish Hall, and the purchase and furnishing of the new Presbytery in Sussex Gardens, meant that the parish had incurred a considerable debt, which it was the task of Father Kevin and his successor to pay off. When Father Kevin came to the parish there were two collections at each Sunday Mass, and a collection at Wednesday's Mass. After a discussion with the Advisory Council, these were reduced to one collection at Sunday Mass. This in fact resulted in a higher income – a sign of a mature and responsible congregation!

Early in 1979, Father Kevin received a phone call from Archbishop Michael Bowen, asking if he was willing to take over the parish of Whitstable by arranging a straight 'swap' with Father Denis Barry. He agreed, and the exchange took place on 21st February, 1979.

31. Father Denis Finbarr Barry

Father Barry came of Irish parents. As his father was a regular soldier in the British Army, his family moved from place to place. As a boy in Woolwich, he felt a call to the priesthood,

Fr Denis Barry

and entered St Joseph's Junior Seminary at Mark Cross. Small in statue, but full of energy, he excelled in football, hockey and cricket. When he moved on to St John's Seminary, there were two Denis Barrys, so he was called 'Finbarr.' In his last year at Wonersh he was Dean of Students, an office he bore calmly and modestly. Ordained in 1951, he served as Assistant Priest at Burgess Hill, Tonbridge, Gravesend, Hove, East Grinstead and Dartford. He was appointed Parish Priest of Plumstead Common, and then to Whitstable. He was a keen fisherman, and on arrival at Birchington as parish priest in February, 1979, he said that the Archbishop had moved him from Whitstable because he had fished the waters there, and now he could try his luck in the sea off Birchington.

There was still a debt incurred by the building of the new Parish Hall, and there were costly defects in the Church itself. Father Barry would often be seen on the roof with some of his parishioners, patching holes or cleaning gullies. Jumble sales, summer fêtes, quiz nights, dinner dances and other fund-rising ideas were the order of the day; everyone was involved and lots was achieved, through the varied abilities of the congregation. But the membership of the UCM was decreasing, as younger mothers were no longer joining, and in the early 1980's the UCM was discontinued.

Soon afterwards, a new group, called the Ladies' Circle, began to meet monthly, under the chairmanship of Eileen Bonsor, and was always willing to organise or help with various social and fund-raising activities.

Father Barry was still living in Sussex Gardens when there was an attempted burglary at the church. The Archbishop urged him to live back 'on the premises', the decision was made to build a new presbytery, and Mr Robin Carter (who later became a Permanent Deacon) was chosen as the architect. Father Barry was concerned that the trees on the chosen site might make it difficult to obtain planning permission, so a group of parishioners, with a chain saw and a digger, set about clearing the land.

The New Presbytery

As the new presbytery was being built, and costs mounted, parishioners decided to save money by decorating it themselves. When the house in Sussex Gardens came to be sold, house prices had escalated, and the parish was able, therefore, not only to repay the loan from the Diocese, but to help considerably with the cost of the new presbytery.

Father Barry was a well-loved pastor, and left a happy and united parish when he resigned after a quintuple heart by pass, and retired to Ireland. He left the parish, not only free from debt, but with a substantial sum on loan to the Diocese. Gerry Andrews was his devoted housekeeper. In Ireland, he said, he felt "unwanted and useless", and asked his successor, Canon Clements, if he minded his returning to live in Birchington. His reply was, "Welcome, so long as you keep a low profile!" This he did, but was always ready to help out as a local supply priest. He kept in touch with the sick and housebound in the parish, and continued to visit them.

In later years he became increasingly forgetful and confused, and eventually unable to say Mass alone. In his last year, he calmly and cheerfully told Canon Clements that he had Altzheimers disease, with only a year or so to live. He said farewell to the parish on 3rd May, 2008, and died peacefully in his sleep on 3rd January 2009, at St George's Retreat, Burgess Hill.

32. Canon William Clements KHS

From now on, this history is written in the first person (singular and plural).

Canon William Clements KHS

I was born in the parish of Earlsfield, in South London, and educated by the Salesian Fathers at Battersea. After three years as a Clerical Officer in the Board of Trade. I served four and a half years in the Royal Navy during the War, and then studied for the priesthood, first at Campion House, Osterley, and then at St John's Seminary, Wonersh, where I was ordained by Bishop Cyril Cowderoy on 30th May 1953. I served as Assistant Priest at Epsom, Peckham Rye and

West Greenwich, and then for ten years as Administrator of St George's Cathedral, Southwark, first under Archbishop Cowderoy and then under Archbishop Michael Bowen. This was followed by ten years as parish priest of Abbey Wood and Thamesmead. Thamesmead was a local Ecumenical Project where four congregations, Catholic, Anglican, Methodist and United Reformed, shared one building. Then, in 1990, I came to Birchington. I arrived on Thursday, 6th December, 1990, to find luncheon, prepared by Grace Brewer, on the table. What a nice welcome to a warm and comfortable Presbytery.

1991

On 3rd January 1991, I invited Mr Andrew Clague, our architect, to lunch, to have a preliminary discussion about work in the Church. The roof needed attention, and everyone was telling me how cold and damp it felt. Forty-eight people attended our first Parish General Meeting, and had their say. Matters discussed included the Sign of Peace, Children's Liturgy, girl Altar Servers, Servers' Vestments, a Repository, and Hymns at Mass. I announced that we had £51,000 on loan to the Diocese, plus £6,500 in our Current Account. At a second Parish General Meeting, Mr Andrew Clague was present, and proposed inserting a damp course in the walls of the church a wooden floor built on joists over the present concrete floor, plus gas-fired central heating for both church and hall. It was agreed that a survey and costing should be undertaken. We decided at that meeting that all our altar servers should wear albs and red girdles, instead of cassocks and cottas. These were worn for the first time on Easter Sunday, 1991.

Gwendolen Foster, a greatly loved parishioner and sacristan, died on 31st March.1991, aged 84. Her younger sister Dorothy, then aged 81, took over. The Knights of the Holy Sepulchre, of which I am a member, came to Mass on 26th April.

Our first Parish Pastoral Council was elected on 21st April. The members were - Denis Murray (elected Chair) Sheila Baugh, Eileen Bonsor, Stan Brennan, Grace Brewer, Tom Conway, Stan Delamere, John Mann, Charles Mara and Anne Miller.

On 21st April, ten parishioners, chosen by me, were commissioned by Bishop Howard Tripp at Aylesford as Special Ministers of the Holy Eucharist. Their primary task is to take Holy Communion to the sick and housebound; they also administer the chalice to the faithful at Mass. Those I chose were: Stan Brennan, Tom Conway, Dorothy Foster, Daphne Harris, Eddie Hughes, Mary Joslyn, John Mann, Anne Miller, Denis Murray and Sean O'Donnell.

On 3rd June our Bible Study Group met for the first time. They still meet, at 3.00 p.m on Mondays, to discuss the Scripture Readings at the following Sunday's Mass.

The Archconfraternity of Saint Stephen, founded about 1901, has as its aims and objectives:-

1. *To encourage the highest standards of serving at the altar in the Church's public worship.*
2. *To help servers to understand the ceremonies, and so grow in reverence and prayerfulness.*
3. *To unite servers in different parishes and dioceses for their mutual support and encouragement.*

On 14th July, 1991, the Archconfraternity was established in the parish of Birchington, and a document to this effect, signed by Cardinal Hume, is framed in our sacristy. The following servers were enrolled.:- Men: Sean O'Donnell, Eddie Hughes,

Tom Conway, Terry Brewer and Charles Mara. Boys: Mathew Webb, Richard Carré, Andrew Mason and Sean and Kieran Newton. Our MC, Stan Brennan, was already a member.

On that same day, we accepted the tender of Messrs W W Martin Ltd for £23,386.72 plus VAT and costs for roof repairs, insertion of a damp course, laying of a new timber floor on joists, and the installation of gas-fired central heating for both Church and Hall. From Messrs Cox & Son of Ramsgate, we ordered a carpet for the whole Church. Mother Concordia of Minster Abbey, assisted me with the choice of colour. We laid lots of carpet squares on the floor of the shop and eliminated all but two. Mother Concordia prudently stepped back and left me to make the final choice of Almond Green. All the work was completed by 28th September. The Abbot of Ramsgate, Dom Bernard Waldron. joined us for a special Celebration Mass and Social Evening on 5th October.

On the same day we took part in the first Thanet Deanery Forum, held at Holy Cross School, Broadstairs, where 130 people, with their clergy, discussed the needs of the local church in Thanet, and sought to prepare a Pastoral Plan for the future. Father Peter Soper, then parish priest of Margate, deserves praise for organising several such annual gatherings, and also some Deanery Social Events.

On 14th October Bishop John Jukes presented the papal medal 'Benemerenti' to Dorothy Foster, in recognition of a lifetime service of church and community as nurse, catechist and sacristan.

Our first Mass for the Sick, Disabled and Housebound took place on 1st December. Eleven received the Sacrament of the Sick, eighteen parishioners provided transport, and Eileen Bonsor arranged for a Red Cross Ambulance. The joy on the faces of our special guests, some of whom had not been to church for years, was our sufficient reward. It is now an annual event.

At our Parish Council Meeting in December we were already discussing the re-ordering of the sanctuary. We also decided to have an occasional Latin Mass in the Tridentine Rite, with the Archbishop's permission. The first took place on 19th July, 1992. 58 people attended; George Downar was our organist, and Brendan Farrow our cantor, as we sang the Proper of the Day, as well as the 'Missa de Angelis.' Three such Masses were held, but attendances dropped, and those attending were from other parishes, so we quietly abandoned the idea.

The total cost of work done on the church during the year was £44,609.15. Owing to the generosity of the people (including legacies) we were able to do all the work without going into debt.

1992

As our works of charity, we had agreed to support a Junior Seminary at Kilema, in the diocese of Moshi in Tanzania. In January 1992, we sent our first cheque for £408. "Now I can give my students meat twice a week," said the Rector in his reply. In preparation for the forthcoming General Election, Rev Canon Norman Baldock, Vicar of St John's, Margate, arranged three inter-denominational meetings to question the three candidates for North Thanet.

On the Feast of Pentecost, all the churches of Birchington combined for a Service of Prayer for Christian Unity, held that year at the Methodist Church.

On 14th June, Eddie Hughes, retired Head Teacher of St Gregory's School and daily Mass-goer received the Medal of

Merit of the Archfraternity of St Stephen for Altar Servers, in recognition of 66 years of service as an Altar Server.

On 28th June, a coach left after the 10.30 a.m Mass for our Parish Outing. We had lunch at Aylesford Friary, took part in the Outdoor Procession of the Blessed Sacrament at Lesnes Abbey, and ended with tea as guests of my former parish, St Paul's, Thamesmead. Our Church was full to overflowing for the funeral of John Mann, a greatly loved parishioner who had served the local church well for over forty years. He died on 7th July, aged 74.

Award of long service medal to Eddie Hughes

This summer, Christians of Birchington had agreed to visit one another's churches to "Come and See." Seventy of them came to our church on 13th June to hear from me an explanation of our customs, and traditions and a tour of the church, followed by tea in the Hall.

On 18th July, about 100 attended the Baptist Church for the same purpose. Visits to other churches followed. A new Sound Amplification System was installed in our church by Messrs Smye-Rumsby during 1992. In August, with the approval of Bishop John Jukes, and the agreement of our Parish Council, Father Axious, a priest of the Coptic Orthodox Church, celebrated their liturgy for the first time in our church. The ceremony took nearly three hours, amid clouds of incense. For several years they continued with a monthly liturgy, until they were able to purchase a redundant Methodist Church in Cliftonville.

Constance Mary Jarman died on 25th October. She was married in our church in 1927, and spent the rest of her life in Birchington. In Father Charles' time she was his housekeeper, cleaned the church and was a daily Mass-goer. In November we began our first of a series of Courses on "On Sharing our Faith" with Birchington people who had expressed interest. These courses have continued, and a number of people have been received into full communion.

We were well represented in Canterbury Cathedral on 14th November, 1992, when 1100 Catenians and their families from all over the British Isles, attended a Mass celebrated by Archbishop Michael Bowen. Denis Murray (President of Province 7) read a lesson, Tom Conway was a Steward; Stan Brennan, Sean O'Donnell and Matthew Webb were among the Servers and Sue Laurie was a Cantor.

1993

Girl Servers | First raised at a Parish Meeting in 1991, this subject came up again at Parish Council Meeting in May 1993, and it was decided to have a secret ballot on the question, "Would you agree to have Girl Servers if they asked?" The Parish Council agreed that we should not disobey Rome, or our own Archbishop, but that I should raise the subject at a Deanery Clergy Conference, with a view to it being referred to the Council of Priests. The matter was raised, but deleted from the minutes! However in August, 1994, I announced that Rome had agreed to admit girls and women as Altar Servers. Having consulted the local Fire Service, the Parish Council implemented their recommendations. It was noted that the maximum seating accommodation of our Hall was 156 persons.

We decided that, in future, the Patronal Feast and the Anniversary of the Dedication of the Church should be celebrated together on the Sunday nearest to 11th July, but making sure it did not clash with the celebration of St Mildred at Minster. I did some research and reported that 49 of our children attended Cathedral schools, but 53 did not. On 18th September we held our first Churches Together in Thanet Sponsored Walk for the Homeless, and raised £7,410.

1995/6

For over forty years the flat roof of the church had presented problems, and in January, 1995, the Parish Council recommended unanimously that we should ask the architect for an updated report.

New roof under construction

Mr Clague was in favour of a new pitched, tiled roof, and estimated the cost at £23,000 plus VAT and fees. The Parish Council agreed to ask parishioners for interest free loans of £1,000 each. By May we had received £6,500 in gifts, plus promises of another £14,300. In view of the adverse report which Messrs Stanley Hicks & Son had made to Father Williams, the architect decided to consult the Lawrence Hewitt partnership, structural engineers, who advised the underpinning of the sub-standard foundations at the north-east corner of the church, in order to cope with the 25% extra weight which the new roof would add. This was done. The tender of Messrs W W Martin & Co., excluding the tower and a new ceiling within the church, was accepted, and work commenced. To help repay the loans we had obtained, the Parish Council agreed to the setting up of a Building Fund, with a target of £80 a week. The work was completed in February, 1996, and involved 49 timber trusses and 35,000 pantiles. The total cost was £38,000 plus vat, plus fees of £6,742. A debt of £12,300 remained owing to parishioners who had made loans, but in 1996 Leslie Fitt, a loyal parishioner who lived in great simplicity, left a legacy of £28,000 to the parish, and on 15th September, 1996, I was able to announce that all loans had been repaid.

Our Hall was redecorated in the summer of 1995, and new curtains were purchased. Our 4th Deanery Forum, on the subject "Sharing the Good News with the whole community," was led by Father Oliver McTernan, parish priest of Notting Hill, on 14th October, 1995.

1996/7

Patrick Drane, a faithful parishioner, died on 5th January, 1997, aged 77, and left us a legacy of £30,146.

A fire door was installed at the end of the Servers' Sacristy.

A parishioner, James Galbraith, repaired and repainted the exterior of the Church Hall, charging only £70 for materials. The Hall Roof felt covering was completely replaced by Messrs Mullaney at a cost of just over £3,000. The Hall was then in use by the Birchington Bridge Club, an Irish Dancing Class, regular Whist Drives run by Win Sturton, and by the Isle of Thanet Historical Society, as well as for parish functions organised by the Social Committee. The Church Garden also received some attention.

Members of the Ladies' Circle, who were doing so much to help with refreshments at Social Functions, had urged us to refit the Hall Kitchen, and, at a cost of £2,332, an MFI Malmo Kitchen was installed. To cope with all this work, a Finance and Works Committee was instituted, made up of James Galbraith, Ron Mogavero and Gordon Goward.

Bishop John Jukes made a Visitation in 1997, and recorded that he was well pleased with the work being carried out in all sections of Church and Parish Life. This year, for the first time, Girl Altar Servers were introduced.

Owing to a misunderstanding over dates, Bishop Jukes was unable to carry out our Confirmation Service, and my friend, Bishop Francis Walmsley (retired Bishop of HM Forces) kindly came to our rescue, and confirmed Jennifer Goward, Alexia Cooke and Fay Elliot on 9th October, 1996.

1997/8

Another legacy, this time from another devoted parishioner, Horace O'Donnell, of £11,000, prompted us to invest £6,000 in a Memorial Fund to help young people of the parish to further their education. This could cover uniform and books, school journeys etc.

Mr Gwyn Derrick produced a plan for re-ordering the Sacristy to provide some storage space and more convenient working conditions. This was executed by the Pine Furniture Company at a cost of £718.

A portable Repository, to our own design, was made and is now in use.

Mr James Naden, a local builder, replaced the dilapidated wooden fence around the Presbytery Garden with a six foot brick wall, at a cost of £4,426. The Finance & Works Committee inspected the contents of the two floors of the Church Tower, and decided what items should be retained for use, sold, repaired or discarded.

A Memo on Guidelines for Health & Safety was received from the Diocese, and voted upon. 'No Smoking' signs have been put up in the Hall. This year saw the inauguration of our Junior Parish Council, which still meets about once a month. Oliver Egan, aged nine, never at a loss for words, said to me one day in 1997, "Canon Bill, why don't we have a Junior Parish Council? You consult grown-ups about what they think. Why not consult the children too?" This got me thinking and I wrote forty-one letters to all known young people in the parish between the ages of nine and fifteen.

Eleven of them came to the first meeting and three others sent letters of apology. I explained to them that their role would be like our Senior Parish Council – and I would look to them for advice. They had ideas, suggestions and offers to make. One youngster suggested that I get a roving microphone so that I could move around the church when I am giving my homily. Another said that part of the homily should be addressed specially to the young people in the parish. Another youngster asked for benches for the children at the front of the church so that they can see what is happening in the liturgy. They asked for a children's section in the weekly parish bulletin. And, they offered to weed the church grounds.

Mathew Goward, 11, was elected chairman, and Hannah Newton, 10, was elected secretary. Her hand written minutes, on one page of A5, were models of brevity. It was agreed at the start that chairman and secretary should hold office for only six months so that everyone would have a chance to play these rôles. This was in 1997, and we met monthly thereafter. When I bought the microphone they had suggested, they asked me how much it cost and they decided to have a special second collection to pay for it. Paul Monaghan, Mathew Goward and Katie Burney each spoke at one of the Sunday Masses and they raised double the usual second collection for our small parish.

At Christmas time that first year, they roped in their friends and formed a choir for our festival of lessons and carols. With the confidence they gained, they organised a summer concert to raise money for charity. Ian Gregory, then aged thirteen, produced a script, complete with stage directions, for a one-act farce, which he directed and produced himself. Other members and their friends offered, or were persuaded, to sing, dance, recite poems, tell stories and play music. Oliver Egan was elected as compère for the concert of twenty-one items. They have had three such concerts and have raised nearly £1,000 for various charities – all chosen by the children.

One Sunday morning, the twins John and Eleanor Coverdale, aged seven, approached me and asked how old they would have to be to join the Junior Parish Council. I told them that they'd have to be nine years old; but at the next meeting, the members decided by secret ballot to lower the age to seven. They argued that it is better to change the rules than to break their own rules.

About twice a year, we have a Mass for the children of the parish, i.e., a Mass totally geared to the children. In 2006, John Coverdale, then aged fifteen, produced a draft of a liturgy for our Easter Sunday Mass. There was to be only one reading, the Gospel, we would use the Apostle's Creed instead of the Nicene Creed; the children would write and read the bidding prayers; they would all come and kneel around the altar during he Eucharist Prayer. Incense was to be used – but I had to explain the reason for using it. The draft included several other short explanations of what was happening in the Liturgy, and these would be read by children. John's draft was discussed by the members of the Council at two meetings, it was amended and, after I checked the guidelines given in the Directory for Masses with Children that only one reading was permitted, it was finally approved.

Their ideas are not all centred around the liturgy. The Junior Parish Council challenged the Senior Parish Council to a quiz night (which the Junior team won).

At one of our meetings, a visiting teenager from a local youth club asked the members what the fundamental purpose of the Council is. Hannah Newton told him in no uncertain terms that it was to make the church better.

I have been astonished at how much we have achieved, how much fun we've had and how much I have learned by listening to those young people. It is amazing what has come up in the course of discussion. Angela Walker, a grandmother, who is not related to any of the children, sits in on the meetings and she, too, has her say. Members have made it clear that they do not want parents to be present as it inhibits free discussion. When Bishop John Hine came on a pastoral visitation, I left them alone with him and they had no inhibitions talking to him about their rôle in the parish.

Some former members are now at University. At sixteen,

young people are eligible for the senior Parish Council, and James Osborn and John Coverdale were so elected. An account of the Junior Parish Council was published in the 'Tablet' on 25th April, 1978, and another on 20th January, 2007. As the sale of Catholic papers was running at a considerable loss, it was decided to discontinue this service and to encourage parishioners to order their copies by post.

There were now eighteen Altar Servers. Some were enrolled in the Guild of St Stephen, and Mr Charles Mara received the Silver Medal in recognition of his faithful services since 1960. To add to the splendour of our 10.30 am Mass, six torches were made, to be carried in by torch bearers during the Eucharistic Prayer.

Requiem Mass for my brother Arthur, on 11th November, 1998, was followed by his interment at Minster Cemetery. Arthur flew with the RAF during World War II, and afterwards for British Eagle and Dan Air.

Junior Parish Council 2003

1999

The idea of a Men's Circle grew within the Parish Council, and I invited 47 to a dinner, with myself as host, on 22nd January 1999. 29 accepted, and Alun John was the caterer. After circulating the wine, I gave them all a list of jobs that needed doing, and called for volunteers. The result was poor, but one good result was that they agreed to meet every couple of months for dinner, with myself as guest, and Tom Mitchell as convenor. Louis Clarke and Tony Lyle, as cooks, produced an excellent three course meal, with sherry reception and a glass of cognac to finish, all for £10 a head. We even invited guest speakers, including Father Wilfrid McGreal O.Carm., and Sister Alice Montgomery, OSU. On other occasions, I threw in a topic for conversation at the coffee stage. Later in the year, I invited 76 ladies to dinner and 40 came. I thanked them for all their support.

The re-ordering of the sanctuary was twice discussed by the Parish Council. They and all the people had always insisted that the tabernacle should remain in its central position in the sanctuary. On 4th November, 1999, I placed before them my plan, with a model I had made, and this they approved in principle unanimously. But I still needed the congregation to agree, as well as the Diocesan Art & Architecture Committee.

Traces of woodworm were found in the church benches, and even in the panelling. John Hammond dealt with the problem thoroughly and effectively.

On 19th December, Bishop John Jukes presented the following medals to our altar servers:-

- *A Bronze Medal to Gregory Burney, who could now serve Mass alone.*
- *A Silver Medal to Matthew Cocklin, in recognition of ten years faithful service.*
- *A Gold Medal to Louis Clarke, who had completed 60 years as an altar server.*

Anthony Hawes, the National Secretary of the Archfraternity, was present. At the same ceremony, the Bishop blessed our new

Gold, silver and bronze medals

Johannes 20 organ, recommended by our organist Tim Attride. It cost £8074. The old organ, which had given thirty years' service, was donated to the Ursuline College for tuition purposes.

2000

In September, 2000, Mr Andrew Clague, our architect, offered us three options for the reordering of the sanctuary:-

Option 1 | Remove the old high altar, reredos, tester and steps, and build a permanent stone altar, so placed that the celebrant could celebrate Mass facing the people, and walk right round the altar. Build a stone ambo for the Liturgy of the Word, and a stone plinth for the tabernacle, placed in a new apsidal chapel built on to the front of the church. Estimated cost £43,475.

Option 2 | As in option 1, but without the apsidal chapel built on to the front of the church.

The architect suggested, instead, moving the panelling, and building a 'false' wall eighteen inches in front of the rear wall of the sanctuary, with an archway, and suitable lighting, to create the impression of a special chapel for the Blessed Sacrament Estimated cost £27,050.

Option 3 | Leave the sanctuary as it is, and make no change.

At all Masses one Sunday, I asked the people to vote for their choice. The result was:-

Option 1	27 votes
Option 2	43 votes
Option 3	34 votes
Total	**104 votes**

The Parish Council took the view that 70 were in favour of change, and recommended Option 2.

2001

In January, 2001, Option 2 was placed before the Art and Architecture Committee, who voted in favour. Archbishop Michael Bowen then gave his approval, and work commenced. The stone used for the new altar, for the ambo and for the plinth for the Blessed Sacrament was purchased from the Dean and Chapter of Canterbury Cathedral, and was cut and installed by their workmen. It is the same stone as that used in

New altar being put in place

restoration work on Canterbury Cathedral today, and comes from a quarry in Normandy at Lépine, quite near to Caen, whose quarries provided the original stone for the Cathedral. The high altar, a metre cube of solid stone, weighs 2½ tons, and a gantry had to be erected to put it in place. The re-ordering was completed on 19th October, 2001.

2002

The new altar was solemnly consecrated by Archbishop Bowen on 17th April 2002. The following accounts of the ceremony, written by two of our altar servers, were published in the *Southwark Diocesan Liturgy Bulletin*.

Church interior with new sanctuary

THE ALTAR'S BIG DAY
by John Coverdale (aged 11)

"On Monday 15th April 2002 a practice was held for the altar servers involved in the consecration of the new altar and blessing of the new ambo. We met His Grace the Archbishop's MC at 7.00 pm to sort out which part each person would play and what would happen. Once the run-through had finished everyone went home feeling happy about their part in the ceremony.

On Wednesday 17th April 2002 all the servers were at the church by 7.00 p.m. After putting on my alb, and lighting the church's consecration candles, I went with Martin Brennan, the book bearer, and Eleanor Coverdale, mitre bearer, to the presbytery to meet the Archbishop and get ready.

The other servers arrived at the presbytery. Charles Tarelli (cross), Charles Mara (thurifer), Ashling Kealy (boat), Oliver Egan (acolyte), James Osborn (acolyte), Alexander Osborn (holy water bearer), Louis Clarke and Stan Brennan (assistant MC's). We then processed into the church with Archbishop, priests and deacons to the hymn 'Christ is made the sure foundation.'

After greeting the people, the Archbishop blessed some water and sprinkled the altar, servers and people whilst we all sang 'Spirit of the living God.'

Next he blessed the ambo. The readings were read by Mrs Bernie Coverdale and Mrs Monica Moulsdale and then the six cantors sang the Responsorial Psalm. The Creed was sung in Latin as it was a special occasion. After that it was the Invocation of the Saints in which twenty-eight saints names were read out as we asked them to pray for us. This list included Saint Florentius and Saint Urbicius. Then it was the Invocation of Christ and then supplication for various needs.

Then came the important bit: the relics of Saint Florentius and Saint Urbicius were cemented into the altar. The Archbishop placed the box, which had been sealed with a wax stamp and containing the relics, the saints' names and the date on which the ceremony was performed, into the altar. We sang the very appropriate hymn 'For all the saints' whilst the stone-mason, who had helped carve the altar, sealed the hole with a stone block and cement. Most of the priests and deacons were trying to get a good view, even wanting to help! The stone mason finished just as the last verse was coming to its end - perfect timing.

After the Prayer of Dedication the altar was anointed with Holy Chrism which is Holy Oil. The Chrism was poured on to the altar by the Archbishop. He poured and rubbed it into the altar, first in the centre, then on all four corners. Whilst he was doing this we sang 'The Spirit lives to set us free.'

After the excess oil had been wiped off the altar, a brazier of burning charcoal was brought up the aisle. Into this was put quite a great quantity of incense which produced a lot of sweet smelling smoke. Canon Bill was told 'We couldn't see each other at the back!' Paul Moynihan, the Master of Ceremonies, then took the brazier off so that Cynthia Macdonald could place the new altar cloth on the altar, candles could be placed on the altar in their new holders and the sanctuary could be decorated with flowers. Meanwhile we sang 'Peace is flowing like a river.'

Once the hymn had finished a deacon was given a lighted candle by the Archbishop and he lit the candles on the altar and by the tabernacle.

Afterwards the Mass proceeded as usual with the Liturgy of the Eucharist followed by the Communion Rite, the Final Blessing and the Recessional Hymn which was a rousing 'Now thank we all our God.' We were all invited to a party in the Church Hall after the ceremony. During this His Grace the Archbishop and Canon Clements each made a short speech.

I thank Canon Bill for having the sanctuary re-done and giving me the opportunity to take part in this incomparable ceremony which I enjoyed tremendously. It was a great honour which I shall remember for the rest of my life."

Church exterior with new roof

A SMALL PART IN A LARGE CEREMONY
by Alexander Osborn (aged 9)

"As I was a server at the Mass for the consecration of the new altar I had to arrive half an hour before the Mass commenced. It was all quiet and plain and you could hear the organist practising. It felt as if there was about to be a special service happening. My alb had been washed specially and I put this on with the other servers who were chatting like geese. I filled up the holy water bucket with water and processed with the other servers over to the presbytery where we waited for the Archbishop, priests and deacons.

When the Archbishop came out of the presbytery I felt nervous because the Mass was starting and I felt as if I would drop the water vessel. It was crowded when we came into the church and the organist started playing the entrance hymn. It felt different, being an evening service and I worried because I wanted to do well. Canon Clements looked proud because the Archbishop had come to his own little church.

The Mass started and I went to my seat. The Archbishop stood before the altar and I was given the signal to bring the water to the Archbishop. I brought up the water, which he blessed, and then sprinkled the altar and ambo with it. He went down the church and sprinkled the congregation with the holy water. I felt sad when I gave the water vessel to the deacon because my little job in this big ceremony was over. But I had done it well.

My favourite parts of the ceremony were listening to the homily because the Archbishop made us really think about the altar and how we would be lost without it. The incense on the altar was impressive because it came gushing out of the brazier, filling the whole church.

At the end of the service I felt sad because I had enjoyed this lovely ceremony and, of course, it will never happen again. I processed out of the church and I went and took my alb off before going into the hall to join the guests. When I was about to leave I wanted to say goodnight to the Archbishop so I went to the Archbishop and said, 'Goodnight Archbishop.' He replied, 'Hello. You held up the water vessel for me. You were very good and you will remember this, won't you?" 'Yes, I will, Archbishop,' I said. We walked home in the dark and I felt that I had really enjoyed this beautiful, memorable occasion."

On Good Friday 2001, I woke to find that the 5 foot figure of Christ on our Calvary had been destroyed during the night by vandals. Pieces were later found on the beach at Minnis Bay. It took a long time to find a replacement, but on 21st December, 2002, the new Calvary was solemnly blessed by Bishop John Hine. A Loop System for the hard of hearing was installed, at a cost of £363.

2003

On being appointed as Organist and Choirmaster of All Saints Church, Tim Attride, who had been our organist for many years, had to resign. On 6th March, 2003, we welcomed Ann Shufflebotham, as Organist and Choir mistress.

At our 1993 Annual General Meeting, we formally agreed to a 'No Smoking' ban on all our premises.

Several celebrations marked the Golden Jubilee of my ordination to the priesthood by Bishop Cowderoy on 30th May, 1953. On Tuesday, 27th May, 2003, Archbishop Michael Bowen invited all Golden, Ruby and Silver Jubilarians to concelebrate Mass with him at St Georges Cathedral, and to join with him for luncheon afterwards.

On Wednesday 28th May, members of the "Wonersh 1953 Class" met at Birchington for a Mass together at 12 noon, followed by a splendid luncheon in the Parish Hall provided by the ladies of the parish. This group includes two bishops, as well as the widows of three classmates who left us during the six year course at Wonersh.

On Friday 30th May, I invited priests of my Support Group, together with other priest-friends and Birchington clergy of various denominations, to a Mass of Thanksgiving in our church at 12 noon, followed by a luncheon served by caterers.

Re-ordered Sanctuary in use

On Sunday, 1st June, at 6.00 pm Bishop John Hine joined us for a Parish Celebration Mass, followed by a Social Gathering in the Parish Hall, during which I was presented with several gifts, including a cheque for £2,000.

On Tuesday, 17th June, the nuns of Minster Abbey invited me to celebrate a Mass of Thanksgiving at 8.15 a.m., and afterwards to join them for breakfast, with flowers decorating my place at table. On Thursday, 17th July, the pupils of Year 7 at the Ursuline College (of whom I was Year Chaplain) invited me to celebrate a Mass of Thanksgiving with them, and presented me with a group photograph, taken that day before I left.

Stan Brennan, who had been our Master of Ceremonies for many years died on 19th October, 2003, aged 71.

2004

In 2004 a toilet for the disabled was installed in the foyer, at a cost of £6000. Our architect offered us various options for a new lighting system for the church. We chose fluorescent tubes placed along the top of the oak panelling, and these were fitted by Mr John Hollett. We then asked Mr John Hammond to extend the oak panelling upwards to conceal the lighting, which he did effectively.

2005

On 31st July, 2005, we celebrated the hundredth birthday of Gladys Birch, who was received into full communion at the Easter Vigil in 1994. Gladys became a daily communicant, organist and Secretary of the Parish Council. She received a Papal Blessing, and we planted a tree to commemorate the occasion. Gladys died, aged 102, on 1st September, 2007.

2006/7

On the recommendation of the Parish Council, a concrete ramp was laid down, to provide wheel-chair assess to the Presbytery, and Safety Lights were installed in the church grounds.

Sister Kate Clapham, Sister Moya Lemmon and myself, having worked together for some years on RCIA programmes, wished to do something to promote mutual understanding, tolerance and respect between different world faiths, all in the cause of peace. So in November, 2006, the Sisters brought together four of us, all local people:- David Gradus, an Orthodox Jew, Jiggy Bhore, a Buddhist lady, Mohammed Ewas, Imam of the local Mosque, and myself, a Catholic priest.

We decided that each of us would give a Talk to the people of Thanet about what we believe, and how it affects what we do. We would be happy to answer questions, but not to enter into argument. We would invite everyone, it would be free of charge, and we would, in turn, provide light refreshments. The meetings would be limited to one and half hours. Each Speaker would be limited to twenty-five minutes, there would be twenty-five minutes for refreshments, and the remaining forty minutes would be for answering questions.

So we advertised in the local churches and the local Thanet press, and the meetings were held on four Wednesdays in May 2007 in our Hall. We had no idea how many would come. We were agreeably surprised when over eighty people came to the first Talk; delighted when one hundred and twenty people came to hear Mohammed Ewas give the final Talk. I was asked to chair three of the meetings, and Sister Katie Clapham chaired my own Talk on Christianity.

For the first meeting I, as Chairman, explained that the purpose of the meetings was to understand each better, and to promote tolerance, and mutual respect, so that we can live alongside each other in peace, and work together for the common good. So we could all ask questions, but not argue, nor seek to score points, nor compare, nor even discuss at this stage. Just listen. A round of applause showed that this was the common mind of those present.

A Question Box was provided, and solemnly opened after refreshments. After all written questions had been dealt with, the floor was open to questions ONLY. Supplementary questions had to be placed at the end of the queue. It all worked out well, and there was a pleasant, friendly atmosphere each evening.

After the last Talk we asked those present three questions:-
- What did you specially enjoy about the Talks?
- Have you any criticisms?
- Have you any suggestions for the future?

We had thirty-eight replies. Listeners generally enjoyed the opportunity to hear from people who genuinely practice their faith, rather than from books – especially in a calm and respectful atmosphere with honesty and openness. It was nice to find we had so much in common. Michael Tilley, aged ten, said, "You've done something good. Be content with that." But more people want us either to repeat the same process, at least once a year, perhaps with different speakers and a different venue, or to arrange discussions with smaller groups. Some members of the Baha'i faith asked to be included next time. How could we involve children and schools? What about social gatherings, and visit to one another's places of worship? What about other faiths, Hindu, Sikh, Salvation Army etc? Invite the press next time.

We four speakers met afterwards to discuss these ideas. We were convinced that it was all worthwhile, and did good. We decided to go gently, to repeat the Talks, perhaps with different speakers, at monthly intervals in the autumn at Hartsdown School, advertising more widely. This eventually led to the setting up of the Thanet Inter-Faith Council.

Alexander Osborn, the fourteen year old Chairman of the Junior Parish Council, commented as follows:-

> "I believe honestly that these talks were quite simply a fantastic and excellent idea. Many people seem to agree with me, as our Hall was full to overflowing with people at every talk. In school, where there are lots of people from different faiths or no faith, pupils in ignorance accuse one another of all sorts of beliefs that they do not, in fact, hold. In school and in the Junior Parish Council (a small

collection of young people from our parish) we try to combat this and understand why this happens, to recognise that at this age we are questioning and to recognise that it does happen. These talks were particularly interesting for me, having learnt about these religions at school, and having this issue often questioned about at school. Not only in school but in a whole community, many of us also question why we are so different and don't get along."

It is important that we understand and learn from other religions just as they do from us, and, from these inter-faith talks, learn to come to work together in our faithfully-diverse society in promoting for everyone the common good. Archbishop Kevin, who is Chairman of the Department for Dialogue and Unity of the Catholic Bishops' Conference of England and Wales, and of its Committee for Other Faiths wrote to me:-

"It is of the nature of Inter-Faith work that it tends to be 'ad hoc' and unstructured. It depends on local contacts and local initiatives. Your meetings seem to have been a model of this, and I commend you for what you are doing."

On 6th October, 2007, I entered hospital for a knee replacement. I was discharged in time for Christmas, but in February, 2008, I had to return to hospital, and remained there for the rest of the year. On 16th February, 2009, Archbishop Kevin accepted my resignation as parish priest of Birchington.

In May, 2009, I returned to Birchington from Coloma Court and on Sunday, 17th May, I celebrated the 10.30 am Mass, seated in my wheelchair. After the Mass I blessed a statue of Saint Bernadette which, through a generous gift of Mary Crow, had been put in place in Our Lady's grotto in the church garden.

33. A Fourteenth Centenary Remembered (1997)

To celebrate the 14th centenary of St Augustine's arrival in Thanet in 597, four outstanding events took place:-

- *A Deanery Mass at St Augustine's Abbey, Ramsgate, on Sunday, 25th May, 1997, celebrated by Cardinal Basil Hume.*
- *An official welcome the same day for fifty pilgrims who had travelled from Rome, following the route taken by Saint Augustine 1400 years ago.*
- *A Diocesan Mass at St Augustine's Abbey, Canterbury, Tuesday, 27th May, 1997, celebrated by Archbishop Michael Bowen.*
- *Solemn Vespers in Canterbury Cathedral that same day.*

Our Lady's shrine with St Bernadette

On Sunday, 25th May, the eight parishes of Thanet cancelled their own late morning Masses, and came together for a Solemn Mass celebrated by Cardinal Basil Hume, Archbishop of Westminster, in the grounds of St Augustine's Abbey, Ramsgate. About 850 people attended, and Stan Brennan, Ian and Charlotte Gregory were altar servers. Concelebrants included Bishop John Jukes, Abbot Lawrence O'Keeffe of Ramsgate and five other Benedictine Abbots, Monsignor Dilwyn Lewis, Vicar Capitular of St Mary Major in Rome, as well as the parish priests of Thanet.

That same afternoon at 3.30 pm, Cardinal Hume, Archbishop of Westminster, the Most Reverend George Carey, Archbishop of Canterbury and Councillor Margaret Davies, Chairman of Thanet District Council, met at Hugin Green, overlooking Pegwell Bay, to welcome officially fifty pilgrims who had travelled by coach from the Church of San Gregorio in Rome, following the route taken by St Augustine. Archbishop Carey then led the pilgrims to St Augustine's Cross, for the short service, and on to Minster Abbey, where the Thanet District Council had arranged a barbecue.

On Tuesday, 27th May, about 8,500 people from all over the Diocese of Southwark came in 109 coaches to attend a Solemn Mass celebrated by Michael Bowen, Archbishop of Southwark, in the grounds of St Augustine's Abbey, Canterbury, close to the original tomb of St Augustine. Birchington supplied the oak altar, together with altar cloths, prepared by Cynthia Macdonald, and a damask silk frontal, probably the work of Father Wilfrid Emery. Concelebrants included Bishops Charles Henderson, John Jukes and Howard Tripp, a number of Benedictine Abbots and about 200 priests of the Diocese. Bishop Jukes was the homilist, and after Mass, English Heritage, who managed the site, encouraged us all to sit on the grass for our picnics.

That same evening, Canterbury Cathedral was packed with hundreds standing, for Solemn Vespers, sung in Latin by Benedictine Monks and Nuns, both Catholics and Anglicans. Their procession, led by cross and acolytes, took a full quarter of an hour, without any pause, to enter, and at the end came Cardinal Hume and Archbishop Carey, walking side by side. At the end of Vespers the whole congregation joined in the 'Salve

Regina.' The ceremony concluded with a sermon by Cardinal Hume, in which he made a strong plea for Christian unity.

34 Our Lady and Saint Benedict Centenary

I am indebted to James Osborn for the following account of the Centenary celebrations:-

> "A Centenary Committee, formed in September 2007, had prepared a calendar of events, which began with a day of recollection at the shrine of St Jude in Faversham on the 21st June, 2008. The day started with Mass served by our altar servers. Father Wilfrid McGreal provided an informative programme and those who attended all ate lunch together and took part in 'lectio divina,' which for some of the younger members was the first time they had experienced this. Twenty-three people attended and there was a view that we should do something similar in the next year.
>
> The parish exhibition (held over the weekend of the 20th/21st July) showed the cohesiveness and the willingness to work together that makes this parish so unique. Much planning and organisation had been put into this event, and its resulting success means that this was well rewarded. The centre pieces of the exhibition were the chalices. It had been agreed at the Centenary Committee and by Canon Clements that it would be appropriate, in centenary year, to refurbish an old chalice that had been in the parish since 1908. Also, it was agreed to have a replica made to celebrate the centenary in 2008.
>
> The money for both the replica, the refurbishment of

the original chalice and to cover the cost of the centenary celebrations as a whole was raised throughout the year starting in Lent, eventually totalling over £5000.

The exhibition also featured a complete history of the parish from its beginnings in 1908 right up to the centenary celebrations. The history was displayed on large display boards and featured mostly photographs provided by the photo albums in the Presbytery and from parishioners. The text was written to supplement the photographs so it was mostly a visual history. It was interesting to see the development of the actual church building in particular, and in fact this display was so successful that it made a return at the Evening Prayer held in November. Also at the exhibition, various vestments were displayed with labels giving explanations as to their use. For some of the younger parishioners, it was the first time they had seen such items as the maniple and chalice veils.

These were displayed on four big tables in the middle of the hall, which in turn surrounded a smaller table on which were displayed the two new chalices and the beautiful and ornate monstrance. Therefore, the new chalices and monstrance could be seen, but not touched! The display of the chalices and the monstrance was decorated with two vases of flowers. Liturgical books were also displayed, which gave some parishioners a chance to reminisce about the days of Mass in Latin!

Also in July, a talk was held in the hall on 'one hundred years of Birchington' presented by local archivist Jennie Burgess. Her talk contrasted 'then and now' in Birchington as well as covering the chronology of our church, covering each of the Priests that have been in charge of the church and the key events during their respective tenures. The talk featured a slide show of photographs, which allowed everyone to see in greater detail and many of these photos were used in the Parish Exhibition. This talk was much enjoyed by those who attended and provoked much interesting discussion and amusement as people remembered and recognised events and occasions from the past one hundred years. On 15th August, the church was full to celebrate the 100th anniversary of the first mass held in Birchington. It was fitting that Abbot Paulinus Greenwood of Ramsgate could celebrate this Mass as it was the Abbot of Ramsgate who celebrated the first Mass in 1908.

September sadly saw a planned outdoor Mass against the back drop of Our Lady's grotto moved inside due to bad weather. However, the weather had significantly improved by the end of the Mass so that prayers were said outside by the grotto. A special liturgy was formulated for this occasion by John Coverdale, and this was presented in a booklet especially designed for this particular Mass.

On 23rd November, the Solemnity of Christ the King, we held a special service of Evening Prayer, to which all the Birchington churches had been invited. Once again, a special booklet outlining the service was produced. The Evening Prayer featured a lot of music, and the presence of the other churches in the congregation meant that the singing was excellent and the general atmosphere joyful.

And so December, and the Centenary celebrations culminated with the Mass to celebrate the 100th anniversary of the first Mass said in our church. Celebrated by Bishop Hine on Sunday 7th December (a day before the actual anniversary), this Mass also saw the much anticipated homecoming from hospital of parish priest Canon Clements. The new chalices were blessed, and a papal blessing was received and hung up inside the church. The occasion was made even more special by the presentation of silver medals for ten years altar serving to James Osborn, John and Ellie Coverdale and Martin Brennan, and bronze medals to Michael Tilley-Dack and Martin Docherty. The altar servers had all contributed in their own special way to making every Mass in the centenary year run efficiently. A special buffet lunch was held and once again this had been excellently organised by the social committee, who had provided refreshments for so many of the events during the year.

The centenary year also featured a party for the children of the parish. This was held on a lovely sunny Saturday in June. The party featured a barbecue, 'gutter' ice cream (an idea borrowed from the Scripture Union Holiday Club, which many of our children attend each summer) and a Conjurer who was excellent in captivating the attention of every child who attended, no matter how old. A special cake designed to look like the exterior of the church was also provided for the children. The children also received souvenir bookmarks with a picture of the church on to commemorate the centenary. The event was much enjoyed by children and adults alike.

A number of items were bought or made during this centenary year which helped to enhance the celebrations.

An oak panel listing the parish priests of Birchington was made and put up at the back of the church above the font, and a visitor's book was also bought.

But perhaps the most visual addition to the church was a purchase of a flag pole and a papal flag. This was flown at most of the celebration masses throughout the year. During Lent, Allison Moores prepared a banner for our centenary which appeared at all the later events. It was based on the mosaic above the church. It made its first appearance at the Good Friday service in the village centre.

In Canon Clements' absence, we had three supply priests from Kenya saying Masses throughout the year. Father Marcos covered us from February through to July, and was amazed on Easter Sunday when it started to snow, as, hailing from Africa, he had never seen snow before! Father Ralphael celebrated Masses from July through to October, and will be remembered for his jovial manner which helped to make the centenary events that he was

Aerial view of Church and Presbytery, 2002

present for even more enjoyable. Finally, Father Boniface said Masses from November to the close of the year and concelebrated at the final centenary celebration on the 7th December. Also during this year the parish said goodbye to Father Denis Barry, who moved from Birchington to Burgess Hill. A farewell Mass with refreshments afterwards took place on 3rd May and it showed again the warmth and friendliness that the people of this parish feel towards its priests and its church."

35. Our Local Catholic Schools

There is no Catholic school in Birchington. Local Catholics have always had to make sacrifices to provide a Catholic education for their children, using various Catholic schools in Westgate, Margate, Broadstairs and Ramsgate. Since 1865 no fewer than ten such schools have been available at different times.

St Ethelbert's School | Soon after the monks arrived in Ramsgate, a small school was set-up in the sacristy of the Abbey Church. Until about 1871, a chapel-of-ease was established in Artillery Road, Ramsgate, and a small school, called St Augustine's School, grew up around it, and was gradually extended by buying up and demolishing neighbouring cottages. In 1894 Sisters of the Holy Family of Bordeaux took over the school. A young French priest Pierre Bienvenu Noailles, founded the "Holy Family of Bordeaux" in 1820, as an Association in which all Christians could follow Christ through the example of the Holy Family of Nazareth, as lay men or women, married or single, Contemplative Sisters, Apostolic Sisters, Priest Associates or Consecrated Seculars. By the time of his death in 1861 the

"Holy Family of Nazareth" numbered 20,000 members.

The Apostolic Sisters used their gifts and talents wherever they discerned a human need, and in their early days one of the great needs was the education of children. The first Apostolic Sisters came to England in 1853, and by 1900 had 15 convents in various parts of Britain. In 1894 they took over and developed St Augustine's School in Ramsgate as a Boarding and Day School for boys and girls. In 1929 the school moved to a new site, with new buildings, in Dane Park Road, alongside St Ethelbert's Church, and became the first Voluntary Aided Catholic Primary School in Thanet. It was solemnly blessed and opened by Bishop William Brown. Older pupils remained on the old site. All pupils were 'evacuated' during World War II. After the war, in 1945, an agreement was made with the Sisters of the Assumption. The Holy Family Sisters could continue to take children between four and eleven in St Augustine's School, while the Sisters of the Assumption would receive older children into their own Boarding and Day School in Ramsgate. In 1965 the name of the school was changed to St Ethelbert's School. The Holy Family Sisters continued to teach there until 1970, when they left Thanet.

St Augustine's College | St Augustine's College began its existence in 1865 as an independent fee-paying grammar school, with a small number of boys living within the monastery. Buildings were gradually acquired, and numbers grew. By 1890 there were seventy pupils. In World War I, zeppelin raids forced the closure of the College in 1917. Then in 1919 the monks decided, instead, to open a Preparatory School for boys up to thirteen years old, and this continued until 1939, when the outbreak of World War II caused the school to be 'evacuated' to Hemingford Grey in Huntingdonshire, where it remained until 1957, with a capacity of eighty boys.

Meanwhile, in 1952 the monks opened a Day School in Ramsgate for local Catholic boys, and in 1957 these were joined by the monks and pupils from Hemingford Grey to form one College. Numbers kept increasing, and in 1960 the monks purchased Assumption House, in Goodwin Road, Pegwell Bay, for use as a Preparatory School. (From 1878 to 1958, the property had been a Convent School run by the Sisters of the Assumption.)

By 1965 there were three-hundred pupils in these two establishments, the College and the Preparatory School. In 1972 the monks purchased Les Oiseaux Convent and its school buildings in Westgate, and the College and Preparatory School moved there.

Competition with local voluntary aided schools made it increasingly difficult to remain financially viable as a fee-paying Independent Grammar School, and in 1995 the decision was made to close Saint Augustine's College, and to transfer pupils to the Ursuline College, which became the Voluntary Aided Catholic College for boys and girls of Thanet.

The Ursuline College | The Ursulines are the oldest and largest teaching order for girls in the Catholic Church. Founded by Saint Angela Merici at Brescia in Italy in 1535, they are now found all over the world.

The Ursuline Nuns at Boulogne-sur-Mer were running a large and successful boarding school, and a free day school, with a history going back to 1634. But in 1904 anti-clerical laws were passed in France, suppressing all religious teaching congregations, and the nuns, followed by forty-five of their pupils, crossed the Channel into exile, and settled at Westgate-on-Sea. Gradually they established a school for girls, and the foundation of their convent was laid by Abbot Bergh of Ramsgate in 1907.

By as late as 1921 most of the pupils were French, and they still regarded their exile as temporary. In 1926 The French nuns left Westgate, and returned to Boulogne. They were replaced by a small community of eight English and Irish Ursuline nuns, led by Mother Frances Lemarchand. There were only seventeen boarders and six day girls, but gradually numbers increased, and buildings were added. The school was 'evacuated' during World War II. The school buildings were requisitioned by the Government, and occupied by the WAAFs (Women's Auxiliary Air Force) based at Manston. When the school returned in 1946 there were one hundred and five boarders and only two day girls. By 1964 the position was reversed, and there were a hundred and nineteen day-pupils and ninety-seven boarders.

In 1995 the monks of Ramsgate decided to close the St Augustine's College for boys (then just down the road from the Ursulines), and in 1997 the Southwark Diocese decided to close Holy Cross School (a Catholic Secondary for boys and girls) in Broadstairs. These two decisions presented a real threat to Catholic education in Thanet, and a huge challenge to the Ursulines, who had decided to establish, in 1995, the co-educational Catholic College of today, with Sister Alice Montgomery as Headmistress. In 1998 the College was granted 'Voluntary Aided' status by the Government, and in 2004 the College, now with over eight hundred pupils, was awarded the status of 'Specialist Sports College.' So the little French speaking 'Pensionnat des Dames Ursulines pour les Jeunes Filles' of 1904 had become in its Centenary Year, the flourishing and increasingly popular Catholic College for boys and girls of Thanet which we see today.

Les Oiseaux | The Order of Canonesses Regular of Saint Augustine was founded in 1597 by Saint Peter Fourier and Blessed Alix le Clerc. The original aim was the teaching of village girls, much neglected at that time. In 1904 the nuns were expelled from their property in Paris in the Couvent des Oiseaux in the rue de Sèvres, by the anti-clerical regime.

They found a house in Westgate, and set about building a chapel and a school which flourished until 1972, when the monks of Ramsgate acquired the property, and moved St Augustine's College on to the site. Some of our older parishioners were pupils there, and remember the Sisters with great affection.

Jim Murphy told me that they also organised a primary school which he attended as a small boy.

Saint Gregory's Catholic Primary School | Salmestone Grange was built by the monks of St Augustine's Abbey, Canterbury, in the 12th and 13th centuries. This chapel, and the monastic buildings, have largely survived, and were, with some surrounding land, given to the monks of Ramsgate by Major H S Hatfeild in 1936. So it was that, in land adjacent to Salmestone Grange, Saint Gregory's School, Nash Road, Margate, was built, and solemnly blessed and opened by Bishop William Brown on Tuesday, 29th August. 1939. It was originally built to accommodate both primary and secondary age pupils, with a school hall large enough to seat the whole school, and large and pleasant grounds.

The first Headmaster was Ken Knight, who remained in post for twenty-five years, until he became the first Head of Holy Cross School, Broadstairs, when it was opened in 1963. He was succeeded at St Gregory's by Eddie Hughes, who remained as Head Master until his retirement in 1975. (On retirement, Ken Knight was ordained as one of the first Permanent Deacons in the Southwark Diocese, and ministered in the Broadstairs parish until he died, aged 86, in 1999. Eddie Hughes, with his wife Mary, made their home in Birchington, where Eddie, after retirement, became a daily Mass server and an active parishioner).

Nine months after the opening of St Gregory's School, World War II began, and the whole school was 'evacuated' to Cannock, in Staffordshire. In the post-war years there were various additions and improvements to the buildings, and in September, 2005, a Nursery Unit was opened. Saint Gregory's School continues to flourish, and is the local Catholic Primary School for the Birchington parish.

St Joseph's Catholic Primary School | The Sisters of the Christian Retreat were founded by Father Anthony Receveur at Fontenelles, in Eastern France, in 1785, as a group of fourteen young women dedicated to a community life of meditation and reflection and the teaching of children. During the years of the French Revolution (1789 to 1792) they suffered persecution and banishment, returning to France in 1804. By 1902 the Sisters had seventeen houses – thirteen in France, four in England, and more than a thousand members. But the anti-clerical laws of 1904 drove them out of France once again and in 1906 they built St Joseph's Convent School, Broadstairs, on its present site.

It was at, various times, a primary school and a middle school, sometimes with pupils up to sixteen years old. In July, 1997, the school closed as an Independent (fee paying) Convent School, and in September 1997 the entire roll was transferred to the state sector, re-opening in the same buildings as St Joseph's Voluntary Aided Primary School, with two hundred and ten places for boys and girls aged four to eleven years. The school continues its good work today, and former pupils living in Birchington have happy memories of their school days there.

Saint Angela's School | To cope with the closure of Saint Augustine's College in 1995, and the transfer of its pupils to the Ursuline College, there was a need to provide for younger boys and girls. In 1998, when the Ursuline College was granted Voluntary Aided Status as a Secondary School, the Ursuline Sisters decided to open an Independent Catholic School, for boys and girls aged four to eleven years, within the grounds of the Ursuline College at Westgate. The school flourished for some years, and an Ofsted Report said, "The school's provision for pupils' spiritual, social and moral development is exceptional." One parent wrote, "We thought long and hard before making this investment in our children's education. It's a decision we haven't regretted for a moment." Sadly, the school was closed in July 2009. Rising costs, the competition of local state-aided nursery and primary schools as well as the national financial recession, had resulted in the school being no longer financially viable.

Daughters of the Cross | The Daughters of the Cross are a Congregation of Religious Sisters founded at Liège in Belgium by Blessed Marie Thérèse Haze in 1833, to identify and deal with the greatest needs of the Church. They founded hospitals, schools, homes for the aged, etc. They came to England in 1862, and established a school for delicate children in Margate, which later moved to Broadstairs, and closed in 1960. The Sisters sold the land and buildings to the Southwark Diocese, who established there, in 1963, a Voluntary Aided Secondary Catholic school for boys and girls.

Holy Cross School | Holy Cross School, Broadstairs, was opened in 1963 by the Diocese of Southwark as a Voluntary Aided Catholic Secondary School for boys and girls, in buildings formerly used by the Daughters of the Cross as a school for delicate children. Mr Ken Knight was the first Head Master. The school had an early history of good and solid development, but it was not a Comprehensive School, and the more academically gifted local Catholic children attended either the two fee-paying local Catholic Schools (St Augustine's College and the Ursuline College), or the local non-Catholic Grammar Schools. Less than half the children attending Holy Cross School were Catholics, and of these only about 5% were practising. The school worked hard to help children achieve their potential within their capabilities, and to provide a Christian and caring ethos. But Ofsted and RE inspections were hard and negative, not seeming to take enough account of the type of pupils the school was dealing with. Holy Cross School became very demoralised.

In 1997, as the school was about to celebrate the 34th anniversary of its foundation, the Diocese of Southwark announced, without prior consultation with the school staff, that Holy Cross was to close, while at the same time the Ursuline College at Westgate was to become a Comprehensive Catholic Secondary School for boys and girls. Holy Cross School closed on 24th July, 1998.

Saint George's Schools | The Faithful Companions of Jesus were founded in 1820 by a French widow, Madame Marie Madeleine d'Houet, at Amiens in northern France, as a religious order devoted to making Jesus known and loved, through various apostolic works, including the education of children, retreats and missionary work. Communities were established in various parts of France, then in Italy and Switzerland. They first came to England in 1830.

In 1913 the Sisters acquired a property in Cliftonville, on the site of the present public library, and opened a school there. In 1920 the school moved into a new building on the present Stella Maris site in North Foreland Road. The school continued successfully until its closure about 1929. In 1937 the Sisters purchased St George's School (formerly a boys' boarding school) on a lovely cliff-top site in Broadstairs and opened it as a Preparatory Boarding School for girls. The school was closed throughout the Second World War (1939-1945), but thereafter continued as a boarding school for young girls, admitting boys as day pupils. Pupils wore a lovely light blue uniform. The school closed in 1974, but the Faithful Companions of Jesus continue their various apostolic works in Europe, Asia, Australia and the Americas.

Assumption House | While St Augustine's Abbey and College were coming into existence, Benedictine nuns wished to establish a contemplative community in Ramsgate, and had commenced building St Scholastica's Abbey at Goodwin Road, Pegwell Bay. They built too ambitiously for their resources, and in 1877 were appealing for funds in the 'Tablet.' But in 1878 they had to sell their property, which was purchased by the Sisters of the Assumption.

The Sisters of the Assumption were founded in Paris by Saint Marie Eugènie Milleret, on the inspiration of the Abbé Théodore Combalot, in 1839. Their purpose was to provide a good general education (not just needlework and housekeeping!) for girls from the middle and upper classes, who would, in time, have positions of influence in society. The Order spread, and their first foundation in England was at Richmond, in Yorkshire, in 1850. They came to Ramsgate in 1878. The girls' school which they established became known as Assumption House, and had a distinguished career from 1878 until 1938, when it closed, as the Sisters were needed for missions in Canada and Tanzania. The property was sold to the Benedictine monks of Ramsgate for use as a Preparatory School for boys.

Part Four
WHAT OF THE FUTURE?

36. The Same Church

Jesus Christ founded one Church, and one only. Solemnly, at the Last Supper, he prayed "that they all may be one, as you, Father, in me, and I in you, are one." He also commanded us all to "love one another, as I have loved you." Then he took bread, and said "Take, eat, this is my body, given for you." Then, over a cup of wine, "Take and drink, this is the cup of my blood, which will be shed for you." In so doing, he linked what he was doing at table with what he would do on the Cross, and invited the disciples to share with Him in this sacrifice. Then he said, "Do this in memory of me." The Catholic Church has always understood that, in the Mass, Jesus is present really and truly, but mysteriously, continuing to offer that sacrifice, and enabling us to join with Him.

The Mass, the Sacrament of unity, holds the Church together, and has always been seen as essential to her life. Just before He ascended into heaven, Jesus commanded us "Go and make disciples of all nations." That is our task, and the biggest impediment is our disunity. We are a 'divided Christendom.' So, has the unity that Christ gave us been lost? The Second Vatican Council (1963-1965) gave us this answer:- 'unity subsists in the Catholic Church as something that can never be lost.' As we, Christians of various denominations, come together in our search for unity, we all come bearing gifts, and can learn from each other.

I put it to you, dear reader, that the Catholic Church comes offering the gift of unity, together with the gift of authority, necessary, as in a family, for unity, especially in a world-wide family of different cultures. The Church also offers unity down the ages. 'We Catholics,' wrote Hilaire

Belloc, "are at home in all the past of Christendom." St Peter and St Paul both emphasised unity as a precious gift, to be safeguarded.

The previous chapters of this book have presented this unity and continuity as a local historical fact in Birchington and in Thanet, visible and tangible. It is the SAME CHURCH founded by Christ, built upon the apostles and their successors, worldwide and full of variety, as we find in the little church of Our Lady & St Benedict in Birchington.

St Peter, first Bishop of Rome, and his successors, St Linus, St Cletus, St Clement, and the rest of the Popes down the centuries to Pope Benedict XVI today, have been holding the Church together in unity, and, in Our Lord's own words, 'strengthening the brethren.' St Justin, the martyr, who died about 150 AD, defended the faith to the Emperor, describing the Mass in a way recognisable by Catholics today, and affirming the Real Presence of Christ, God and man, in the Eucharist. It was Pope St Eleutherius (175-189 AD) who sent missionaries to the British, with the result that there were British Bishops at the Council of Arles in 314 AD.

It was Pope St Gregory the Great who, in 597 AD, sent St Augustine and his monks to convert the English to Christianity, bringing the same Church, the same faith, the same Sacraments, the same teaching and the same Scriptures. It was St Theodore, Archbishop of Canterbury, who organised the English Church, and supported the nuns of Minster.

It was St Mildred, Abbess of Minster, who witnessed to the Gospel by her life of prayer and her love for the poor of Thanet. It was St John Fisher, Bishop of Rochester, and

St Thomas More, Lord Chancellor of England, who died in defence of that same faith, along with hundreds of others. It was people, like the Crispe family, who kept the faith alive during centuries of persecution. It was priests like Father Thomas Costigan who ministered to a scattered flock. It was the religious sisters, of various congregations, who came, as exiles from France, to teach children and to care for the poor. Then came what Newman called the 'Second Spring' of the same Church. Benedictine monks from Monte Cassino established the parishes of Thanet, and today the parish of Our Lady and St Benedict offers the same faith, the same Sacraments, the same teaching and the same Scriptures to all who will listen. It is the same living Church, growing and developing, as Christ promised when he said, "I will be with you always, yes, to the end of time."

It has not always been easy. The Church is perfect in Christ, her Head, but very imperfect in her members. Even in New Testament times, there were groups which broke away, because they could not accept apostolic teaching. When Jesus Himself unfolded his promise of the Holy Eucharist, many of his disciples "left him and stopped going with him." And so on, down through history, groups and even whole churches, have broken away – the Coptic Orthodox Church, the Greek and Russian Orthodox Churches, the Armenians, the Arians, the Manichees and the Churches of the Reformation. There have been all sorts of reasons for breaking away, and human error on both sides. Political interference, truculence of those in office, misunderstandings, intolerance, greed and stupidity all played their part. Many of those who broke away were good and sincere people, holy people, and there was much truth in what they held. The Church is a living Church, and has always been in need of reform (semper reformanda). But that reform has to come from within (as in any family). There has always been, and must be, variety within a worldwide Church. Pope Saint Gregory the Great wrote, "Where there is one faith, a diversity of usage does no harm to the Church." But that one faith has to be guarded and cherished, and the Church held together in that faith.

In the search for Christian unity, as we shall see in the next and final chapter of this book, we must be prepared really to LISTEN to each other, to admit past mistakes, and to change.

We all come bearing gifts. The Catholic Church offers to all that gift of unity, which 'subsists' in her as something which has not, and cannot, be lost. The Catholic Church claims to be the original Church, founded by Christ, and having Christ as its Head; built on St Peter and the Apostles, and alive and active today throughout the world; the SAME CHURCH, "reeling but erect" in the words of G K Chesterton. In all humility, and giving all the credit to God, we offer that gift of unity to all people of good will.

37 Christian Unity

Jesus founded one church, and one only. He prayed that we would remain one. Yet we are divided. In Chapter 18 I listed "Other Churches in Birchington," and spoke of our efforts as fellow-Christians to be friendly, to meet together, to listen to and to respect each other, and to work together.

This has been a gradual process, at least from the time of Father Wilfrid. But is this enough? We are still separate and divided. Are we content with that, or is there a real will to come together, and to be one church? The stages in ecumenical growth have been identified by one writer as follows:-

> ***Confrontation***
> ***Competition***
> ***Co-Existence***
> ***Co-Operation***
> ***Covenant***
> ***Commitment***
> ***Communion***

These are not, of course, watertight divisions; one shades off gradually into the next. We rarely change our attitudes suddenly; we need time to think and to adjust ourselves to experience. As individuals, and as communities, each is somewhere along that road, or, maybe, has not yet started!

I was present at a Conference of three hundred and thirty Church Leaders of over thirty denomination, held at Swanwick, in Derbyshire, in 1986. Cardinal Hume made a decisive intervention, which included these words:-

"We should have in view a moving, in God's time, to full communion, a communion that is both visible and organic." He recognized that, in such communion, there would not be uniformity, but legitimate diversity. Within the Catholic Church there has always been considerable diversity, but we need, as Catholics, to agree about the essentials of our faith, about the nature of the Church, about morality, about the Sacraments. And then, as a matter of urgency, we need to explore these beliefs together, with our fellow Christians, and listen to them. We all come bearing gifts as we meet together, and we must listen to each other, and learn from each other, and be prepared to change. Pope John Paul II, in his encyclical "Ut unum sint," set a good example of being open to change. He sees his office as Bishop of Rome to be a ministry of unity, and asks all the Churches "to seek together the forms in which this ministry may accomplish a service of love recognised by all concerned."

But where can dialogue go, where participants have said in advance that they cannot advance from absolutist positions? I think that the answer is to do what we can, and see our search for unity as a journey towards God. Christian Unity is a mystery. In my own ecumenical journey I have learned a few lessons:-

Lesson one | UNITY FROM STRENGTH

Christian Unity is going to come from a position of strength, not weakness. We must feel secure and firm in our own faith. The better we know and explain our beliefs and feelings to each other, the more likely are we to understand one another, to reach agreement on essentials and to accept, with tranquillity and joy, great variety in non-essentials. It is ignorance which breeds insecurity, and the feeling of being threatened by the differing beliefs and practices of our separated brethren.

Lesson two | TENSION

The commitment will involve tensions, sacrifice, and sometimes even suffering. There is tension between my act of faith in my Church's' teaching, on the one hand, and my commitment to work for Christian Unity on the other. They are like two poles, seeming to pull me apart, as I cling to them as poles of a mystery. The truth lies in reconciling those two poles. Unity is a mystery.

Lesson three | Honesty and Openness

We have to be prepared to be very honest with each other, taking the advice of Saint Peter, "Always have your answer ready for people who ask you the reason for the hope that you have. But give it with courtesy and respect." (1 Peter, 3,verse 15). We have to be able and willing to say how we feel about God, and about our beliefs, and about each other. It is not enough to say what we believe, but we must say how we feel. And we must be able to listen, and hear, and understand, and sympathise with the feelings, as well as the beliefs, of others. Why the emphasis on feelings? Because we have inherited our divisions. They are 'in our blood.' They are often irrational, but they are there. We have deep-rooted traditions, family loyalties, emotional attachment to old ways. We have inherited stories of past persecution, hatred and injustice, sometimes within living memory, sometimes very real even today. These feelings need to be brought to the surface and recognised before they can be overcome. This is uncomfortable, but it has to be done. A process of 'healing of memories' can help.

Lesson four | Recognising Goodness

In ecumenical dialogue, we are meeting with people who sincerely love God, and are seeking to do his will. On our part, we must recognise their genuine love, their sincerity and their earnest seeking after truth. We should recognise, too, not only that we believe much in common, but that they have things to teach us too. Our own faith can be deepened by our contacts with them, and our own search for the truth can deepen and widen.

Lesson five | PATIENCE

Because feelings are so deep, we can hurt each other, even unintentionally. There can be setbacks, and we shall be tempted to give up the struggle to 'run back into the herd.' We need great patience, we need to remind ourselves that unity is God's will, and must be worked for.

Lesson six | COMMUNICATION

Work for Christian Unity should not be a side issue; the private hobby of a few enthusiasts. It is Good News, to be spread abroad, but we must be honest, admitting failures, as well as proclaiming successes, and speaking of hopes and disappointments, ideals and frustrations. Sometimes, through misunderstanding, even our own people may accuse us of watering down the faith, betraying the heritage handed down to us at the price of the blood of the martyrs, and so on. We must go on communicating, explaining ourselves patiently, over and over again.

Lesson seven | STUDY

Various 'Agreed Statements' between different Churches have sought to express common ground. They ask for a considered response from the Churches. They are the fruit of immense labour. Yet little interest has been shown by ordinary members. It would be a pity if all this patient study and discussion were ignored or wasted!

Lesson eight | PRAYER

Last, and most important, is prayer. Prayer is the raising of mind and heart to God. Prayer is a loving conversation with

God. It is listening to God, as he speaks to us in the depth of our hearts, but also in and through other people and events. We shall never keep going, and never achieve the goal of unity, without prayer. It is so easy to lose heart, and to give up when faced with difficulty. It is so difficult to be honest with ourselves; to face unwelcome truth; to be ready to change ourselves. Only if we keep our inner eye clear, and our heart full of love for Christ and His Church, shall we achieve that unity for which He prayed, and gave his life.

What of the Future?

Christian Unity is a mystery. How it can be achieved is known only to God. But it involves us all being totally faithful to Christ; striving to be all that he wants us to be, each following his conscience. I pray that the people of Our Lady and St Benedict Church, along with their fellow-Christians in Birchington, may move along the path from co-operation to covenant, from covenant to commitment, and thus to full communion. If we really seek Christ together we shall find ourselves one. May our children live to see that blessed day.

ACKNOWLEDGMENTS

I acknowledge, with gratitude, the help I have received from the following persons in writing the history:-

Mr Kevin Docherty
who, in 1983, provided the first history of the parish.

Dom John Seddon, OSB
archivist at St Augustines Abbey, Ramsgate, for searching through copies of the Thanet Chronicle and the Thanet Catholic Annual for items concerning Birchington, and making photocopies for me.

Miss Jennie Burgess
archivist for Birchington, for her help and encouragement.

Mother Nikola & Sister Benedict
nuns of Minster, for their valuable help.

Mr Jim Murphy
a parishioner who lived his whole life, from 1920 to 2007 in a house in Epple Road, for his reminiscences.

Mrs Faye Stevens
for her patience and hard work in typing from my hand written account.

The illustrations in this book come from a variety of sources collected by me and others over many years. As I cannot trace the originators of this material may I take this opportunity to thank them for the use of their material in my book.
Canon William Clements, July 2010.

BIBLIOGRAPHY

The History & Antiquities, Ecclesiastical & Civil, of the Isle of Tenet in Kent.
John Lewis MS London, 1723

The Parish of Our Lady & St Benedict, Birchington. A Brief History.
Kevin Docherty, 1983

A Brief History of Minster Abbey.
Mother Concordia, OSB 1987

Saints Austin & Gregory Roman Catholic Church 1797-1997.
Father Peter Soper

The Ville of Birchington, its History and Bygones.
Alfred T Walker (3rd Edition) 1991

Woodchurch, Isle of Thanet Archaeological Society 2000.

Historical Insights into Kent.
Joyce Draper 2000

Kent Recusant Historical Society, vol. 2 no 5, Winter 2000.